PiECES
OF ME

Pieces of Me

JESSICA BAILEY

(In their eyes, I live)

Dylan Soklich

Pieces of Me by Jessica Bailey

Copyright © Jessica Bailey 2025

All rights reserved. Without limiting the rights under copyright reserved above, no part of this publication may be reproduced, stored in or introduced into a retrieval system, or transmitted in any form or by any means (electronic, mechanical, recording or otherwise) without the express prior written permission of the copyright holder concerned.

NO AI TRAINING: *Any use of this publication to 'train' generative artificial intelligence (*AI*) technologies to generate text is expressly prohibited. The author reserves all rights to license uses of this work for generative* AI *training and development of machine learning language models.*

Typeset in Sabon and Acumin Pro

A Cataloging-in-Publications entry for this title is available from The National Library of Australia.

ISBN 978-0-6456069-4-2

10 9 8 7 6 5 4 3 2 1

Disclaimer

This book is a personal account of events surrounding tragic losses. It is written from my perspective and reflects my memory, feelings, and understanding at the time.

This story is rooted in truth, however certain names, identifying details, and circumstances have been changed to protect the privacy of individuals involved.

This account is shared with respect and consideration for the individuals and families involved, and all readers. It is my hope that this story brings insight, reflection, and understanding, rather than harm.

Any resemblance to real persons beyond what is publicly known is coincidental.

DEDICATION

Dylan's passing was a moment that shook me to my core.

The news arrived as a phone call that forever altered the course of my life. It was a change that I can only describe as transformative, leading me down a path of understanding and acceptance that I never thought possible. In retrospect, I can't help but feel that Dylan's life and passing were intertwined with my own journey in a way that transcends mere coincidence.

Dylan Soklich was here, and I am eternally grateful for the impact he has had on my soul. This book is a testament to that.

This book is dedicated to Dylan, whose departure allowed me to finally confront the trauma and fear that haunted me for so long. It stands as a testament to the lessons learned, the fears faced, and the peace that eventually emerged from the darkness.

CONTENTS

The Shadow 13
Boogieman 19
Mud Hut 29
Pain 37
Gain 45
The Good Thief 51
The Long Road 63
La-La Land 69
Bad People 75
The Phone Call 81
We are Fools 95
Alone 103
Mission Accomplished 109
Calling 113
Life & Meaning 117
Afterword 121
My Piece of Him—A Father's Reflection 127

CHAPTER 1:
THE SHADOW

THE NIGERIAN SKY above Obi-obeti village hums with the distant drone of an airplane, sending ripples of excitement through the group of young children gathered near a dusty road. The rare sight of a mechanical bird gliding through the heavens represents a world far beyond our reach, filled with unimaginable wonders.

Airoplane go se num bread o!

Airoplane go se num bread o!

These simple words carry the weight of our collective dreams—a plea to bring back something as magical as bread, which we seldom see. We chant in unison, our voices high with anticipation. Barefoot and clad in underwear worn almost out of existence, we sprint after the plane, kicking up clouds that swirl around us like a thick fog. Dust clings and mixes on our sweaty skin, mixing with the earth, but we don't care. We are a pack of wild, exuberant kids, driven by the thrill of the chase and the possibility that if we run fast enough, we might catch up to that distant dream.

Our voices grow louder, more urgent, as the plane begins to fade into the distance. Some of the younger ones start to fall behind, their legs too short, their breath too shallow to keep up the relentless pace. They drop one by one, collapsing into the dirt, but the rest of us are determined. I am seven years old, pushing forward with my bigger cousins, fuelled by a fierce determination to see this chase through.

As the airplane becomes a tiny speck in the sky, the last of us finally slow, our breaths coming in ragged gasps. We realise that we are now standing in the middle of Obi-obeti Primary School, miles away from our homes. With our hands on our knees, we look at each other with a mix of exhaustion and triumph. The plane may be gone, but for a few glorious moments, we believed we could catch it.

THE SUN STILL hovers high above, casting long shadows on the ground. It's hide-and-seek time. Everyone scatters to their hiding spots except for those taking their turn chasing. We play until every ounce of energy is spent, the sun sinking lower with each passing minute. The first pangs of hunger begin to gnaw at our bellies, signalling that it's time to go home. The group disbands, each of us turning towards our own house, leaving behind the echoes of laughter and our dusty footprints.

I am approaching a small compound when I spot my mother in the distance, her silhouette etched against the dying light. She's just arrived back from work on a farm. My younger brother is strapped securely to her back, his small body swaddled in a colourful wrapper. My second brother is on the way, his presence evident in the swell of her belly beneath the sweat-soaked pink dress that clings to her skin. On her head, she balances a large bundle of wood, tied together with frayed ropes. A folded cloth sits between her head and the load, offering what little comfort it can. The weight of it strains her back, which is evident in the slow, measured steps she takes, each one a battle against exhaustion. For a moment, I fear she might collapse, but she continues. Finally, as she reaches the compound, she lets the wood slip from her shoulders with a dull thud. She stands there for a moment, breathing heavily, her hands resting on her hips as she tries to recover from the long, gruelling walk.

"Mummy, welcome," I greet her, my voice soft with admiration.

"You've been doing what you know how to do best?" Mummy's voice cuts through the air, stern and knowing. "Ifelunwa," she says, using the name she gave me, "look at your feet. Before I see you next, you must have had your shower." She continues talking as I shuffle toward the corner, hoping she doesn't notice anything more.

I hate the shower. The thought of cold water sends a shiver down my spine, but there's no escaping it. Mummy never misses a chance to remind me, as if cleanliness is the only thing keeping the world together. Despite her exhaustion, she begins to prepare our evening meal. The last light of day slants through the small, cracked window, casting long shadows across the room as she bends down to arrange the wood she's just carried. Her hands move with practiced rhythm until a fire crackles to life, small flames licking the dry wood. The orange glow casts a warm, flickering light on her face, illuminating every line etched into her skin, each one telling a story of hardship and perseverance. She places a battered pot over the fire, its metal sides blackened from years of use. Smoke mingles with the rich aroma of ingredients as she begins the familiar process of making dinner.

I marvel at her strength, how each task is a step toward holding our world together. I've seen her do this countless times—walk miles with heavy pots of water balanced on her head, feet bare and calloused, trudging through the mud and rocks without a word of complaint. Her back arches under the weight, yet she never stops, never hesitates. Father is away, studying in the city—I barely remember him—leaving Mummy to carry everything alone. She's the ground beneath our feet when it feels like everything else in the world is crumbling.

*

The scent of okra soup with fresh fish slowly fills the small room. It's a comforting smell, one that makes our stomachs rumble in anticipation. We gather around the pot in the centre of our tiny kitchen, the *eba* hot and sticky in our hands. We push the *eba*'s smooth grains together with our fingers and use it to scoop up the thick soup, licking every finger clean with each bite. Our mother splits the fish between us carefully as a final treat to end the meal. The taste of the fresh fish is a luxury we don't often have, and we savour every morsel.

With the last bite swallowed and the rising moon casting a silvery glow over the yard, we dash back outside to the sandpit of our front yard, our bellies full and spirits high. The air is cool against our skin, a welcome relief after the heat of the day. The night is alive with the sounds of our village: the chirping of crickets, the distant bark of a dog, the soft rustling of leaves in the breeze.

*

We sit in a circle, the adults joining us as they tell their stories. Firelight flickers across their faces as they spin tales of White people, their voices filled with a mixture of awe and exaggeration. We listen, wide-eyed, as they describe the White Man as someone who never farts, and planes as massive birds that could swallow our village whole. I can't fully grasp the scale of what they describe, but it doesn't matter. The stories are magical, filling our minds with images of distant lands and unbelievable wonders. They wrap us in a cocoon of fantasy, and we gladly let ourselves be carried away.

When the adults run out of stories, we move on to games. "*Kpa kpa ko lo, kpa ko lo, kpa kpa ko lo, kpa ko lo, odu du me, ogene...*" We sing in chorus, our voices rising and falling in rhythm as we hold hands and spin in circles. The world becomes a blur of movement and sound as we twirl and jump, losing track of time. We are caught in the joy of the moment, our laughter ringing out into the night, carried away on the wind.

Mummy sneaks towards us with her cane, her face stern and movements swift. A sharp lash on my back sends the group scattering, our playtime abruptly ending. It's her way of reminding us that the day is over, it's time to sleep. If it's not Mummy, it's an aunty, someone like Mama Ashim. Someone always watches over us, making sure we don't push the boundaries too far.

Nights in the village are long and restless. The silence wraps around everything, like damp heat that clings to my skin. Only the occasional cry of an owl pierces the stillness, giving me the shivers. Sometimes the wind rustles in the palm trees, their fronds whispering secrets I dare not listen to. The stillness isn't peace—it's a warning, a reminder of the things we don't talk about.

Less than three hundred metres from our front door, row after row of graves stretch across a cemetery. The dead are our neighbours. Every breath of wind carries their weight past the place where we sleep.

Inside, I lie stiffly between my worn mat and a blanket that's too thin, my eyes fixed on the cracked ceiling. My heart races as my thoughts drift to the one thing I can't escape.

Somewhere out there, dead people are locked in boxes and buried in the bush, alone in the dark.

I can't stop thinking about them.

What happens when people die? Where do they go? Are they cold? Are they scared?

My chest tightens, and I whisper into the darkness, *"I don't want to die."*

I sit up slightly, peering into the dark corners of the room, half-expecting to see a figure emerge from the shadows. Each time the darkness creeps closer, I clutch my blanket tighter, as if its threadbare edges could shield me from the unknown.

CHAPTER 2:
BOOGIEMAN

THE LOUD, PANICKED cries of neighbours cut through the air, sharp and sudden, making the hairs on my arms stand up. A coldness creeps into my heart that seems to steal away the warmth of the sun. The adults appear as if by magic, moving swiftly. Their faces are grim, their voices low and hurried, the usual calm replaced by a tense urgency. Mummy is among them.

I huddle with other children in the corner of the yard, our wide eyes filled with fear and confusion. We're too young to understand exactly what is happening, but we can feel the shift. The laughter and joy that had filled the air just moments before are gone, replaced by a heavy silence that seems to smother everything around it. Even the animals sense the change. The chickens stop pecking and stand still, their heads cocked to one side as if listening. The goats bleat softly, their usual lively energy subdued. It's as if the entire world is holding its breath, waiting for something to happen. We aren't allowed to come close, aren't allowed to ask questions. All we can do is watch, helpless, as the adults whisper and cry.

*

I stand in the kitchen doorway which creaks when I open it. The walls, shiny and silver, usually glimmer with warmth, but now they feel cold and uninviting. Okra in the pot bubbles quietly, almost as if it's trying not to be noticed.

Mummy looks different today. She sits alone by the fire in our little zinc kitchen. Her eyes are unfocused, as if she's looking through the flames and into something far beyond and her shoulders sag under an invisible weight. I want to ask her what's wrong, to understand the sadness that seems to hang around her like a dark cloud. The words get stuck in my throat, too heavy to push out.

"This life is truly nothing," she whispers, her voice so soft I almost don't hear it. It's as if she's talking to herself, her words floating away before they can fully sink in. I don't understand what she means, not really. But the way she says it, with such quiet despair, makes my heart feel strange, like it's too big for my chest.

*

The next morning, I wake up to loud wailing. I peek out the door, just a little, so no one will see me, my heart pounding.

There's a group of men walking down the road, their footsteps slow and heavy. The men's faces are downcast, their expressions a mix of sorrow and resignation. They're carrying a coffin painted with blue and white dots, the colours cheerful and bright against the sombre scene.

The box is held by ten men, five on each side. They also carry shovels, the wooden handles worn smooth from years of use. I've seen shovels before, but these feel different, like they're carrying a secret too terrible to be spoken aloud. The crying grows louder as the men walk by, heading toward the thick bush across from Grandpa's house, where the river winds through the trees. I watch them until they disappear into the forest, my feet cold and my mind spinning with questions.

Later, I see the men again. They're coming back, but the box is gone. I run to the door to look closer, to see if maybe I've just missed it, but there's nothing. The shovels are covered in red sand now, which clings to the metal like a memory that won't let go. The men still look sad.

Where did the box go? Why are the shovels dirty? Questions buzz in my head like angry bees, but there's no one around to answer them. The adults' voices are low and muffled through the walls of the house. I'm back in the doorway, questions swirling in my mind. The world has changed, and it has taken something away that we can't get back.

Death is no longer just a story told in hushed tones; it's here, now, moving among us. It doesn't knock—it barges in, leaving grief in its wake. Wails have tripled in volume, tearing through the air, raw and piercing. They start low and build into a crescendo that makes my stomach churn. Sometimes, the cries are so loud, my appetite disappears. The untouched *eba* sitting in front of me grows cold as the news spreads: someone else has been taken.

Eventually Mummy tells us that the beans have been poisoned. Her voice is barely audible, but her words explode in my mind. She explains that chemicals in the beans are killing people. I freeze with half-eaten food in my mouth. Beans are the one thing that always feeds us. I think we're all going to die.

The news spreads slowly, from mouth to mouth. By evening, the air in the village feels changed. Women gather in clusters near their compounds, their voices hushed but urgent. Children play

PIECES OF ME ♥ JESSICA BAILEY

nearby, unaware of the gravity of the conversations happening around them. I stay close to Mummy, watching the lines on her face deepen.

That night, the burial songs begin again. They grow louder, their mournful tones weaving through the village, covering each house like a shroud.

I'm sitting on my mat with the blanket pulled tightly around me. The kerosene lamp sputters and dies, plunging my space into darkness. My breath catches and my hands tremble as I leap upright. "Mummy!" I call, but my voice barely carries over the sound of the rising wind.

I scramble to the door, yanking it open just in time to see her shadow disappearing into the night. "Stay inside," Mummy says without turning back, her voice firm and distant.

The door shuts, leaving me feeling alone in the darkness, even though my siblings are in the room. I shuffle back to my mat and curl into myself, pressing my hands over my ears to block out the burial songs. They're relentless, seeping through the walls and the roof.

Morning comes, grey and muted. The village is still, the air thick with the smell of damp earth and something bitter. I sit outside near the fire pit, staring at the empty space. Mother appears. Her face is pale and her eyes are rimmed with exhaustion. I hesitate before asking, my voice small and shaky. "Mummy, can we move somewhere else? Somewhere people don't die?"

She stops, her hands still holding the bundle of firewood she's brought in. Her eyes soften, but there's something else there too.

"Ify," she says gently, using my pet name to soften the blow as she sits down beside me. "There's no place where people don't die."

Mummy always has the answers, always knows how to make things better. But not this time. I look up at her, realising for the first time that even Mummy, the strongest person I know, is powerless against Death.

The next evening, there's a knock on our door. We're sitting on the floor, dipping our hands into Mummy's steaming okra soup and licking our fingers again. Mummy stands, wiping her hands on her wrapper, and goes to the door.

"It's Okweke," someone whispers.

My heart jumps. Okweke is one of the two drivers we know who travel the long, treacherous road to Lagos. To us, Lagos is another world, full of lights, airplanes, and dreams. Okweke's visits always bring news from that faraway place.

Mummy returns with a sealed envelope in her hands. Her fingers tremble as she tears it open. She reads it silently, a smile slowly spreading across her face.

"It's from your father," she announces, her voice trembling with emotion. "He has a job now! He's sent for us to join him in the city!"

The words hang in the air like a miracle. For the first time in two years, we hear from Father. Mummy's eyes shine with hope as she holds the letter close to her chest.

The news spreads quickly, and soon, my friends are gathering around me.

"You'll get to eat *Agege* bread!" one says, eyes wide with excitement.

"And tea with butter!" adds another.

"There's light in Lagos," someone whispers in awe.

"Ooh, you'll see airplanes. And White people!"

Their amazement makes me feel special. I'm leaving them to join a world they can only dream of.

*

PREPARATIONS BEGIN, a flurry of activity that fills the house with a new kind of energy. Bags are packed, clothes folded with care, and mother's face, usually marked with lines of worry, seems lighter, almost hopeful. For the first time, there is talk of a future beyond the village. I can barely contain my excitement.

*

THE DAY ARRIVES, and we pile into the car—a rickety old thing that smells of petrol and creaks with every bump in the road. It's my first car ride, and my excitement bubbles over, but it quickly turns into a nightmare as the car jolts and shakes over the rough roads. Smells of sweat and petrol fills the air, making me dizzy. I vomit repeatedly, ruining my new clothes and shoes.

"Are we there yet?" I groan, slumping against Mummy. Two days of travel sap all my energy. By the time we get close to our destination, I'm too exhausted to care.

But then I see it. Lagos. The lights twinkle like stars, cars rush by in every direction, and airplanes roar overhead. The city buzzes with life, and for a moment, I forget about everything else.

*

* BOOGIEMAN

Lagos is everything I imagined and more. There is freedom here—a chance to live, to dream, to be a kid in a way that was impossible back in the village. The food is better, the bread is soft and sweet, and the constant hum of airplanes overhead is a reminder that we are in a place where anything is possible.

We settle into a routine, a new normal. Father goes to work each day, his eyes filled with determination, while Mummy runs a small business. We go to school, learn new things, and make new friends. The fear that once gripped my heart seems to melt away in the warmth of this new life.

But the peace is short-lived.

Father falls ill with a headache. I watch as the strong man I've always known is reduced to a shadow of himself. The sickness takes hold and before long, our dreams of a new life in Lagos are crumbling.

The world we had begun building—safety, money, and the promise of education for all of us—is replaced by mounting medical bills. Mummy's small earnings are no match for the financial storm that comes at us. Each day, Father grows weaker, and so does our grip on the exciting new world we had entered.

The decision to leave Lagos is not really a choice. Lagos has pushed us out. The noise, the light, the sweetness and seemingly endless possibilities for our future are gone.

BACK IN THE village, I fall back into old habits, weaving tales of the city that leave my cousins wide-eyed with wonder.

"There's a toilet just for farting in Lagos," I declare with a straight face, watching their jaws drop. "And people don't smile as much as they do here," I add, shaking my head dramatically.

My exaggerations make our short time in Lagos sound like an epic adventure. People hang on my every word, imagining a world they'll probably never see.

Deep down, I know the truth. Death is coming, and it could arrive anytime.

A few days later, an old Toyota grumbles into our broad yard, carrying Father's frail body from the traditional healer's place where Mummy took him, desperate for a cure. But it's too late. As the men struggle to lift Father's limp body from the car, calling for more hands to help, I know what's coming. Minutes later, there it is: the familiar weeping. Only this time, it's my family's room.

Mummy wails. Aunties cry. "Graduate is gone," Mummy chokes, in tears. "I saw him boarding the aeroplane in my dream last night." My heart breaks for her, for my siblings, for myself. The man they call Graduate, my father, was known for his intelligence. Most families couldn't send their children to school, except through a scholarship; Father was one of the chosen few. He worked hard, becoming the top student in the entire state, shattering records and setting his sights on international study. He was the one hope we all shared. We believed he would save us.

The mournful wail I've always heard from afar now echoes through my own soul.

As we gather under the bamboo shade that stands sentinel in front of our yard, each family member steps forward, their faces etched with grief, their eyes red and swollen from days of relentless tears. One by one, they approach the shiny brown coffin where Father now lies in eternal stillness. The once-vibrant man is now encased in this final bed, his body rigid and unyielding.

I stand two metres away, my small frame trembling as my senses are assaulted by a pungent aroma wafting from the coffin—a mix of polished wood, incense, and something unfamiliar that makes my stomach churn.

I can see the worn faces of my relatives, the way their hands tremble as they reach out to touch the coffin one last time, fingers brushing against the wood as if hoping to feel some warmth or some other sign that he is still with us. But there is nothing. It's all cold, hard and surreal, as if the world has shifted slightly off its axis.

The next day, the elders gather in the yard, calling Mummy to join them. Their voices are low and angry, their words like daggers as they point fingers. They accuse her of killing Father, of bringing a curse upon our family. Mummy's tears fall harder, her body shaking with the weight of their words. When they dismiss her, her fate is sealed and my brother, Emeke, is gone.

CHAPTER 3:
MUD HUT

THE STORM THAT arrived with my father's death has deposited us in Isumpe, a village where the road ends. Mummy tells us this is her father's hometown, a place she never thought she'd return to. There is no power here, and the nearest river is fifty kilometres away. But with the help of her uncle, we secure a two-room mud hut—though "secure" seems too strong for a structure with a broken roof and walls that look ready to collapse.

Isumpe is a place where the earth is as dry as our hopes. The Harmattan Wind sweeps the dust of a thousand dry days into the worn-out bricks of our home. Each day feels like a battle against this relentless land which gives nothing without a fight.

*

IN THE MIDDLE of a stranger's farm, I watch Mummy as she wrestles with cassava stems, pulling with every ounce of strength she can muster. The ground is stubborn, cracked and hardened under the sun's unforgiving gaze, but Mummy is more stubborn. She pulls until the roots tear free from the soil with a sound that's almost like a sigh. And then she moves on to the next cassava, as if each is a small victory over the hardships that have followed us here.

I sit in the shade nearby, peeling each cassava as she hands them to me. The task is tedious, but it's work that keeps my mind from wandering too far into the darkness that lingers just at the edge of my thoughts. I keep my head down, peeling and peeling until there's nothing left to peel.

As the sun begins its descent, we load cassava onto the back of our old, worn-out bicycle. Home is miles away, so we must leave now. The bike groans under the weight of us, just as Mother does while she pushes it through the thick sand. We follow behind her. The journey home is a long and tiring one. Seventy kilometres lie between the farm and our hut. We hope to beat the fading sunlight by reaching home before darkness falls, when the path becomes even more treacherous. If we're lucky, the bicycle won't give out on us, leaving us stranded in the middle of nowhere.

The night has swallowed Isumpe by the time we arrive. The houses are scattered and small, each with a roof made from dried palm leaves and walls that creak when the wind blows too hard. It smells like damp earth and smoke from the wood fires that burn in makeshift kitchens around us. Shadows dance under the moonlight, making the familiar path to our house feel mysterious and a bit scary.

*

OUR HOUSE IS small, with walls the colour of mud. Inside, it's dark except for the faint glow from a kerosene lamp. I can hear the distant hum of the grinding machine from the engine centre where Mummy left our loads of cassava. She says it might bring us money in a few days, if the owners pay. Sometimes they do, and sometimes they don't. And if they do pay, it's not much. That's just how things go. Mummy says owning a piece of farmland would change everything for us. She talks about it like it's a treasure we'll find one day.

Mummy is strong. Her arms have lines from all the work she's done—carrying, peeling, planting where she can. You can tell by looking at the veins on her hands that she's like one of those strong trees by the river. She doesn't complain, just keeps going, and people know they can count on her to do the job well.

Our kitchen here is a small area outside with some stones and pots. Mummy starts turning our labour into a simple meal that tastes like a feast after such a long day. The comforting smell of *isege* soup fills the air with the scent of big, fragrant leaves. When the food is ready, we all sit together, crouched over our plates under the soft light. Each mouthful is a blessing and tastes delicious. Mummy only eats a little. She stops before her plate is empty, saying she's had enough. But I know it's because she wants us to have more, to be full. My heart feels heavy. I wonder if we'll always have to struggle this way. I see the sacrifices she makes day after day and wonder if she will ever get to enjoy life.

When the rains come, they bring fresh water and chaos. Our hut leaks, and the mats we sleep on are soaked through. Mummy huddles us in a corner, doing her best to shield us from the worst of it. She places bowls around the room, hoping to catch the water before it floods the entire space. Rain drums on the roof, each drop a reminder of how fragile our shelter is.

When the storm finally passes, she doesn't sleep. Instead, she turns the wrappers she isn't wearing today and all of our clean towels into makeshift mats on the driest spots she can find. She ensures we're laid out comfortably across her colourful skirts, and her eyes stay open, watching over us, always ready to protect us from whatever comes next.

PIECES OF ME ♥ JESSICA BAILEY

I lie awake in the darkness, listening to the sounds of the night; the distant cries of animals, the rustling of the wind through trees, and the soft, steady breathing of my siblings. But it's Mummy's presence that keeps the fear at bay, her unwavering strength a beacon in the night. Despite everything, we're still here, still holding on. And for now, that has to be enough.

*

EVERY DAY IN Isumpe is a cycle that never seems to end: wake up before dawn, work on the farm until our backs ache, eat what little we have, sleep, and then start all over again. School is a memory now, replaced by the hard, endless lessons of survival. Uniforms and fees feel like luxuries—things that belong to a world far from ours. Instead, our hands grow calloused from pulling weeds and hauling heavy loads, and our minds are weighed down by the relentless grind of each passing day.

I know Mummy's heart breaks when she watches us in the fields, knowing there's no classroom waiting for us, and no books to fill our heads with new things. She says we're too clever to waste our days in the dirt, that we deserve to learn things beyond planting and harvesting. She talks about Father sometimes, tells us he was one of the smartest in the state, clever enough to earn scholarships all through his schooling. She tells these stories with a pride that shines in her eyes, even though it's tinged with sadness, too.

Mummy's just as clever as Father was. Everyone in the village says so, and I know it's true. When she reads, her voice is as steady and clear as a schoolteacher's. Her English is crisp and perfect, like she's been to university, even though she only finished high school. She could've gone further, she says, but life had other plans. She got pregnant with me, and university became a dream left behind in exchange for the life we live now.

Sunday is the one day that breaks our rhythm. We set aside the ploughs and the baskets and head to the small church at the edge of the village. The building leans a little, its wooden beams weathered and cracked, and the roof leaks almost as much as ours at home. But to us, it's a sacred place. It's where we pour our hearts out to God, and sing until our voices are hoarse, hoping they will rise high enough to be heard in the heavens. We sing with everything we've got, tears mixing with the dust and sweat that cling to our skin. Our voices shake, raw and desperate as we ask for mercy, for strength, for a better life somewhere down the road. In that little church, we have nothing to hide. We're all the same: tired, worn, clinging to hope.

After the service, we linger in small groups, sharing a few moments of laughter and comfort in each other's company. It's a time to forget, just for a little while, the endless cycle waiting for us back on the farms.

The relief is short-lived. As night falls again and we gather for our evening meal, the weight of our reality returns. We eat together, planning out the week ahead, discussing which parts of the land need to be worked next and which crops are ready to be harvested. Mummy tries to focus, but I see her drifting with thoughts she can't shake. She's constantly reminded that we're no longer going to school, and I know it breaks her heart. Every time she looks at us, I see the regret that she can't give us more. But what can she do? We can't even afford uniforms anymore.

Most nights, there's food on the table, and the cracked roof over our heads offers some shelter. It's more than others have, and I try to find comfort in that. I try to feel grateful, to hold onto hope, but gratitude is a fragile thing when every day feels like a fight.

Mummy says things will get better, but I see the doubt in her eyes, the weight pressing down on her shoulders. While she spends her days worrying about us, I spend mine worrying about her. I fear the shadows will come for her too, that one day she'll push herself too far, and Death will reach out and snatch her away.

It watches from the corners of our lives, creeping closer every time her chest pains strike or her hands tremble from exhaustion. My biggest fear is that one day, without warning, the shadows will claim her, taking her from us before she's ever tasted rest or reaped a single real reward for all her years of labour. We're trapped in this life, in this village, and I don't know how to break free. There's no clear path, no shining future on the horizon. And that means Mummy will keep toiling under the sun, her back bending under the pressure of our need to survive, until the earth itself claims her. It's like a knife in my heart. Every tear she holds back fuels a fury inside me, because I know she's sacrificing everything for us. Every ache, every bruise, every drop of sweat—she pours it all out for us, day after day.

I don't want riches. I don't want luxury. I just want her to be free of this life which is waiting for her to stumble. She deserves to know what it feels like to rest, to breathe without worry, to live without the shadow clawing at her heels. It would shatter me if she left this world without ever knowing that peace.

Her chest pains come more often, striking without warning and sending her to the hospital. The doctors give her half a treatment because we can't afford the rest. The money she earns by wearing herself down for us slips away, swallowed by the hospital, leaving us with barely enough to survive. She can't afford a single day off, unless it's a day spent in a hospital bed, because our meals depend on her relentless will to keep going.

Every morning, as she heads out to the farm, I hold my breath, afraid that today might be the day her strength finally fails. And I don't know how to stop that from happening.

✱

ONE AFTERNOON, AS we're returning from the farm, the sound of a motorbike echoes along the dirt path leading to our hut. It's an unusual sound in a place like this, where motorbikes are rare. We all rush out, curious and excited. The motorbike wobbles its way into our yard, and sitting on it is a man I vaguely recognise: Uncle Patrick, my father's older brother. I have only met him once before, at my father's burial. His presence here feels significant.

Mummy hurries to greet him, offering him a seat and a kola nut, as is customary. But Uncle Patrick politely declines, his face serious. I hover in the background with my siblings, our eyes wide with fascination as we admire the motorbike. It's sleek, shiny, and everything our lives are not. We try to eavesdrop on their conversation, but they speak in low tones, and all we can catch are snippets of words that don't make sense.

But then I see Mummy's face change, her expression crumpling as she listens to whatever Uncle Patrick is telling her. She starts to cry, and my stomach twists with anxiety. I step closer, unsure of what's happening.

Mummy looks at me through her tears. She's barely able to speak, her voice thick with emotion as she finally tells me what Uncle Patrick has come for. He's here to take me away, to live with him and his wife so that I can go to school in a small town. My brother Emeke has been living there, and the hope is that with both of us getting an education, there might be a future for the rest of our family. This could mean freedom for Mummy. I can get a job, start earning money, and finally take her away from suffering here.

Mummy's tears don't stop as she explains. She's already lost so much, and now she's about to lose me too. I feel my own tears start to fall, but I don't want to add to her pain. I try to hold them back, but the thought of leaving her, of leaving my siblings, of leaving this place, as broken as it is, hurts my heart.

Uncle Patrick stands awkwardly to the side, waiting. He knows what this means for Mummy, but he also believes it's the best thing for me. And maybe it is. But as I pack my few belongings and prepare to say goodbye, all I can think about is how unfair it feels.

WHEN THE TIME comes, Mummy hugs me tightly, her body shaking with sobs. I can feel her heart break as she waves us goodbye. I climb onto the motorbike, holding back my tears as best as I can, but the moment we pull away, leaving her standing there, my resolve crumbles.

The wind stings my face, mixing with my tears. The road stretches out before us, leading me away from everything I've known, and most of all, the love of my life: Mummy. I can't help but wonder if I'll ever see her or come back again.

CHAPTER 4:

PAIN

THE MOTORBIKE RUMBLES through a large gate, into a sprawling compound. Towering trees rise up from the earth in a lush oasis that feels like its own world, their leaves creating a canopy of green that seems to stretch on forever. I can barely take it all in—this place is so vast it could be its own village. The narrow road winds its way up to a modest house sitting right in the heart of the block.

I watch, wide-eyed, as we pass trees heavy with fruit: pear trees, orange groves, mangoes hanging low, their sweet fragrance mixing with the scent of cashews and pawpaw. There are so many trees I've never seen before, and I can't help but marvel. I had no idea avocado trees existed here. It feels like stepping into a dream, and with each turn, I find myself falling more in love with the place. Fruits are my favourite thing in the world, and my heart feels at home already.

As we round a corner, my eyes catch a green water bore standing on the right, its steel structure poking out between plants like a silent sentinel. Children are playing nearby, their laughter ringing through the air as they rush to greet us. The bike comes to a slow stop, and suddenly there are three young faces beaming with excitement.

"Daddy, welcome!" they shout in unison, their faces full of innocence and joy. The eldest looks around seven years old, his big eyes gleaming as he runs towards us. But as I lift my gaze, I freeze. There is another child with them: my brother.

Emeke stands much taller than I remember him a year ago, his frame solid and sure. In his arms, he carries a baby, not more than a year old. I smile softly at my uncle's last-born, the one I was told they needed my help with.

We walk together into the house, where my brother gently places the baby down. My uncle's wife stands at the doorway, greeting us with a warm smile. Her eyes are bright with recognition. "Ifelunwa, you're so grown up," she teases, voice full of affection.

As I look around, I take in the simplicity of their home, a one-bedroom apartment with a small parlour, kitchen, and bathroom. Everything is neat and functional, a reflection of the life they've built here. But my brother holds my attention. He's tall now, almost the same height as me. It's strange, this feeling of seeing him here, but I know it's also good to be under the same roof with him. I hadn't realised how much I missed him.

Mummy used to think of Emeke constantly. It seemed like every time she ate, she'd sigh and say, "I wonder if my son is being treated with love." Tears would slip down her cheeks, and the rest of us would try to reassure her that he was okay. I wish I could tell her now that everything really is fine. My brother has found his place here. It's his home now.

*

THE HOUSE IS a beacon in the middle of the night. The power here gives us just enough light to cast a faint glow across the room, creating shadows that stretch long into the corners, while the darkness outside presses against us like an impenetrable wall. The sputtering hum of the generator competes with the sharp, shrill sounds of crickets chirping.

I sit on the couch, my knees drawn up, watching the NTA news flicker on the screen. The words are a blur to me, spoken fast in a language I don't understand, but the sleek professionalism of the news anchors captivates me. Their voices are smooth and confident, like they could command nations with a single sentence. Their clothes are crisp and immaculate, far more sophisticated than anything else I've ever seen. The way they talk and the way they carry themselves feels so distant, and yet so alluring.

Beside me, my uncle sits with his reading glasses perched on the tip of his nose, eyes glued to the screen as though his life depends on it. His fingers tap against the armrest, as if trying to beat in time with the news anchor's words. The world they discuss and their hope for a better Nigeria seems to hover in the air between us. It's a quiet kind of longing, the belief that despite everything, the future can still change. Even though I don't understand most of it, their energy fills the room, pulling me in; a gentle tug on my heart.

Emeke sits at the far corner of the room, bent over his homework. He's been getting excellent results here, and I can see why. The routine he's built for himself is inspiring. It stirs something inside me. Soon, I'll be starting school too, and the thought excites me. In this house, things are different. There's a sense of purpose and a clarity of direction that I long for. There's no such thing as giving up when it comes to my uncle's house. No abandoning hope. They continue to watch and to dream for a better tomorrow.

My brother looks over at me with a silent question in his eyes. I return his gaze, my heart suddenly lighter. His face softens, and

PIECES OF ME ♥ JESSICA BAILEY

he tells me that Nollywood films are on every Friday night at 10pm. I perk up at this. Back in Isumpe, we had no electricity, let alone a television. My knowledge of Nollywood was little more than a memory buried somewhere in Lagos. But now, here, it can awaken again. My pulse quickens with excitement.

Before I get lost in the thought, a knock at the door cuts through the air. The sound is sharp, urgent. A boy around my brother's age bursts through the door. It's Hollyfield, who lives nearby. He's holding a cutlass in one hand and a container in the other, clinking them together in his excitement.

"Are you guys ready?" he asks, eyes shining.

Emeke turns to my uncle's wife, sitting on the other end of the couch, seeking her approval. She nods, smiling. Without missing a beat, my brother springs to his feet. Our 7-year-old cousin, still half-asleep, groggily rises from the couch beside me. Everyone else begins to gather their tools: cutlasses, containers, torches.

"Does your sister want to come?" Hollyfield asks, already halfway out the door.

My brother turns to me, his eyes expectant. For a moment, I hesitate. But then, the allure of the night and the call of the hunt pulls at me. I nod, and we're off.

Outside, the world is reduced to shadows and silhouettes. The constant chirping of crickets fills the air, an ever-present soundtrack to our quiet movements. Hollyfield, Emeke, my cousin, and I, all armed with containers, cutlasses, and torches, move in unison, our footsteps soft on the earth. The ground beneath us is damp, a mix of dirt and scattered leaves, muffling our steps. Each of us navigate our own path through the darkness.

I spot my target first: a small mound of sand surrounding a hole. My heart quickens, and I draw in a deep breath. I raise my torch slowly. At the edge of the hole, a tiny face peeks out. But before I can react, it retreats, disappearing back into the earth. My hand trembles and frustration surges through me. I missed it.

Before I can dwell on my failure, my brother is beside me, his container already heavy with crickets. A smug grin spreads across his face.

"You'll get better with time," he says, voice a mix of pride and teasing. He's done this so many times, and his ease is evident. Every move is deliberate, and he doesn't rush. He knows exactly what he's doing.

I glance at him in the dim light, taking in his presence, the way he moves with such confidence. It's strange, having him so close after a year apart. In my mind, I had imagined moments like this over and over, wondering what it would feel like to see him again. But now, standing beside him, I realise he hasn't just survived here; he's thrived. He's grown healthy and strong, settled, and made this place his own.

I wish I could bottle this feeling and send it back to Mother. I want to reassure her that he's fine. But the distance between us means that this comfort is something I can't share with her yet.

When the hunt finally ends, we make our way back to the house. Crickets are soon sizzling in hot oil, their tiny bodies crackling as they fry. Salt and pepper are sprinkled over them, and the smell fills the air, a heady mix of savoury richness.

In this moment, we are a family, united in a shared experience, the warmth of the house, and the simple pleasure of food. For a while, nothing else matters.

*

PIECES OF ME ♥ JESSICA BAILEY

EACH DAY, I slip further into life here, observing my brother. I slowly come to realise that he has been reduced to a servant. Watching his small hands scramble to keep up with endless tasks, I felt the ache in my chest deepen. I wish that I could shoulder some of his burdens. It's hard not to feel a bitterness that rises like bile when I see him, so young and carrying so much weight.

Saturdays are the hardest. He's the one who looks after my uncle's children—the one-year-old, the seven-year-old, and the other two—caring for them like he's their second parent. He's the toilet cleaner, the one who washes the dishes, the one who cooks, and the one who takes on all the housework. It's painful, watching him this way, knowing that this is the reality that my father's absence has brought upon us. I know Mummy would be devastated if she saw this.

Back in Lagos, we watched Nollywood films that showed young boys and girls doing exactly what my brother does now. Parents wept at the sight, shaking their heads in despair, and I remember Mummy saying, "That would only happen to my children over my dead body." And yet, here we are. My brother is barely nine, but he's living a life that should be reserved for much older souls. I ache for him, but I also know that I'm here to help him. I just hope I can.

*

THAT EVENING, AS I stand at the door holding a small container of salt, I watch my uncle walk in from work. The air shifts, and his children rush to greet him. "Daddy, welcome!" they call out. I stand in the doorway, unsure of what to say. This house is becoming my world. My lips part before I can stop them. "Daddy, welcome," I whisper.

He looks at me, his face impassive. "How are you?" he asks, his voice flat, like it's an automatic response.

From the kitchen, the rich, fragrant smell of *egusi* stew fills the house, stockfish and succulent *tosso* adding a salty, earthy meat aroma that clings to the air. "Where is Emeke?" my uncle calls out, his tone sharp.

I flinch internally, but I don't let it show. Instead, I brace myself.

Later that night, I stand in a corner of the room, my eyes squeezed shut as the sound of the belt whips through the air, hitting my brother's bare skin. *Whack*. The sound is almost deafening. *Whack*. I can feel my brother's pain, even from where I stand. His cries fill the room, echoing against the walls, raw and desperate. I don't move. I can't. I have to be strong. But inside, I feel like my heart is breaking for him.

"How many times have I warned you?" my uncle growls. But the words don't reach me. All I hear is my brother's wail, his sobs shaking the floor beneath us. *Whack* again, the belt landing across his back. He falls to the ground, his body crumpled under the harshness of it all. I can't stop the tears from blurring my vision. I want to run to him, to hold him, to make it stop. But no one is going to help him.

I look at my uncle's children standing in another corner, their faces as blank as their father's. My uncle leaves the room, his belt still hanging in his hand. My brother remains curled against the wardrobe on the floor, his body trembling with each breath.

"Emeke, please take bathing water to the bathroom for me," my aunt's voice calls from the bedroom. My brother's body stills, but he doesn't get up. I walk away from the scene. This is the only chance we have to survive.

CHAPTER 5:
GAIN

SUN POURS INTO the classroom through cracked windows, casting long shadows on the floor. My classmates, forty-nine girls in mismatched uniforms, are lost in their own worlds. I sit by the window, letting my mind drift as the teacher's voice fades into the background. My thoughts are elsewhere.

I think of my brother and I feel a sharp sting in my chest. The sound of the belt slicing through the air, followed by my brother's cries, still echoes in my ears. His bruises, cuts, and endless punishments are all because he's expected to be a grown man at a tender age. I can't understand why.

A tear slips down my cheek, but I quickly wipe it away, reminding myself that this pain is temporary. It has to be. One day, my brother and I will rise above it, and we'll be free from the punishments, neglect, and heavy expectations. School is the only thing that keeps me going. It's the promise that there's more to life than my uncle's house of rules and shame.

I try to listen to the teacher, but the words don't stick. I've learned to block out the noise of reality when it gets too much. It's not easy, but I do it because I know that one day, I'll be someone. One day, I'll have the power to change our circumstances.

It's been two years of surviving and quietly waiting for the moment when things will shift. Now, I'm in my first year of secondary school. It's hard to believe how much has happened in such a short time, but at least there's a goal ahead, even if it feels distant.

At lunchtime, I sit under the mango tree, surrounded by my classmates. I tell them stories of Lagos; of city lights and my dreams. Their attention makes me feel seen in a way that nothing else does.

"You narrate so well," one of them says admiringly. "You make it feel like we're watching it," another praises, her tone filled with awe.

They don't know how much their words mean, how much they feed a fire that has been burning inside me for as long as I can remember. I've always known that I have a gift for storytelling. When I was younger, I would sit in front of the mirror and act out scenes from Nollywood movies. I'd imitate the actors—their emotions, their expressions, their struggles—and perform them with every ounce of passion I had. I didn't watch Nollywood for entertainment; I watched to learn, to absorb everything. I wanted to be like them: strong, confident, captivating.

Now, I tell stories with every ounce of energy in me, adding my own flair to the details. People laugh, they gasp and hang on to every word. This is my escape from the reality I live through every day.

School has become the place where I can hide my pain and turn it into something productive. The lessons are more than just academic; they are tools that will help me build a better future.

Every book, every class, is a small step towards escaping the prison I find myself in, both physically and emotionally.

My father believed that knowledge could change the world, and I carry that torch for him. His death took so much from us, but I carry his beliefs with me: *education is the key to everything.* I will make sure that his sacrifices mean something. Each exam, each assignment, is a chance for me to take control. I feel the weight of my family's hopes resting on my shoulders. I cannot fail them.

I will do everything in my power to make sure that my brother and I share a future where we both have the chance to escape the cycle of pain that seems to follow us everywhere.

SUNDAYS ARE A special treat. We sit on the floor, hunched over steaming plates of fried bean cakes, called *akara,* or homemade warm, comforting *akamu* with rich Peak milk flowing over the top like a river of sweetness. Weekdays bring tea and bread for breakfast—simple but nourishing, a far cry from what we had back home with Mummy. To me, these are the foods of the wealthy, and I marvel at the luxury we experience in this new life.

Still, the truth remains, as do my brother's burdens. The foods we are given cannot mask the bitterness of displacement, family tensions, and our small lives being reshaped by circumstances we didn't choose. Luxury and suffering sit side-by-side here, and I am required to swallow both. It is a strange balance: the flow of abundance and the undercurrent of struggle. And in this duality, I am forced to confront a deeper truth: that even a life of abundance can reshape the way you understand your family and your own place in the world.

PIECES OF ME ♥ JESSICA BAILEY

Here, a part of me can never fully settle. Thoughts of Mummy linger at the edges of my mind. I wonder if she has enough to eat now, like we do. A part of me wishes I could share this bounty with her, to ease her burden and fill her life with the same pleasures I now experience. This longing fuels my determination to succeed, to focus on my studies and finish quickly so that I can return home, armed with the means to provide for her.

The path ahead is clear, and I know that every step I take brings me closer to the day when I can give back, when I can make life just as good for her as it is for me now.

*

At Christmas time, I stare at the spot where my father was laid to rest. The grave that once held a mound of freshly turned earth is now flat, as if time itself has erased the last traces of his presence. The long, rectangular shape is still faintly visible, a silent outline that marks the boundary between the living and the dead. But now the earth has settled and the grave seems ordinary, no longer the raw wound it once was. My Aunt Cele has moved into the property which hosts the mound, her life continuing where his ended. This change stirs something deep within me—a sense of loss that I hadn't fully acknowledged until now.

For so long, a part of me had clung to the impossible hope that Father would somehow wake up. He would rise, shake off the dirt, and return to us. But seeing the earth so undisturbed shatters that illusion. The realisation crashes over me, heavy and cold, that he is gone, truly gone, and there is no coming back. It is hard to breathe.

Inside this house with big hallway doors facing each other, the sounds of laughter and chatter echo through the walls. Cousins gather in the parlour, their voices rising and falling in a familiar fashion. It's a reunion of sorts, but the joy of it feels muffled by my own sense of displacement. I sit quietly on the edge of the room, a visitor in a place that once felt like home.

My cousins, who used to run after the big metal birds with me, crowd around. Their faces are lit up with curiosity. It's been a long time since we last saw each other, and they greet us with a mix of excitement and awe. To them, we are visitors from a different world, far removed from the village. The city we've come from isn't Lagos, the ultimate dream, but it's still a place they can only imagine.

They admire my rubber wristwatch, their eyes wide with envy and wonder. It's simple, but it represents a different life; possibilities that they long for but can't reach. They ask me about the city, about the things we see and do. I answer their questions, but my mind is back at the grave, with what I've lost.

Christmas should be a time of joy, family and togetherness, but this year, it feels different. The house and people are the same, but I am not. I feel detached, a sense of not fully belonging anywhere anymore. The city has changed me, expanded my world, but it has also created a gap between me and the life I once knew. My cousins look at me with admiration, but all I can think about is how far away I feel from the simplicity and innocence of our shared childhood.

As the evening wears on, I remain in the parlour, watching the others as they talk and laugh, their voices growing louder as the night deepens. The festive spirit is palpable, the room alive with the energy of the season. I feel like I'm on the outside, looking in.

I close my eyes for a moment, trying to block out the noise and the memories, but they keep coming back, stronger and clearer with each passing second. Father is gone, the grave is flat, and with it, a part of me has been buried too. But life goes on, and so must I. I just wish it didn't feel so lonely.

CHAPTER 6:
THE GOOD THIEF

LIFE MOVES LIKE an old windmill. Each day begins in the same way: unrelentingly early, the soft greyness of dawn barely spilling through the flimsy curtains as we stir to life. Mornings are predictable: the shuffle of feet on cool cement floors, the clatter of mismatched plates, and the hurried whispers as my brother and I fumble to get ready. The house smells faintly of wood smoke and fried plantain. My uncle's wife, whom I now call Mum without hesitation, is up before everyone else, preparing simple, hot breakfasts to fuel the long day ahead. We rush through our routines, slipping into faded uniforms, our hands busy while our minds wander to the classroom or the fields.

On Saturdays, we belong to the farm, which sits about twenty kilometres from home; a stretch of land with soil so rich and dark it clings to my hands long after I've washed them. It's just large enough to sustain us, with tall cassava plants swaying in the breeze, their leaves reaching for the sky, while corn stalks stand proud, with neat cobs nestled in layers of rustling green. The air is thick with the scent of earth and growing things, occasionally broken by the sound of a bird flitting through the trees that border the field.

Unlike many families in the village who rely entirely on farming for survival, my uncle and his wife are public servants, earning steady salaries that pay for school fees and the occasional bag of rice. This means we farm part-time, working the land mostly for our own consumption.

By mid-morning, the sun is high and unyielding, baking the ground beneath our feet as we hack away at stubborn weeds with blunt cutlasses. Sweat trickles down my back, soaking into my threadbare shirt as I crouch low, freeing the cassava and corn plants from the grip of encroaching grass. My brother works a few metres away, his thin arms moving with determination as he clears his portion. I wonder if he thinks of Mummy as often as I do.

It's been three years since we last saw her. I see her face in my dreams. Her voice lives in my memory. I wonder if she's aged, or if she looks just as she did before. Does she think of us when she's pulling cassava for strangers who'll never care for her pain?

Occasionally, the wind carries the distant hum of a motorcycle or the faint cries of children playing in the village. Despite the exhaustion, there's something deeply satisfying about the work. The smell of strong soil and the feeling of it under my nails are a connection to the land, a reminder that the food we eat comes from our own labour.

As the sun dips lower in the sky, painting the horizon in soft shades of orange and pink, we begin to gather our harvest. Sacks of corn and cassava are heaved onto our backs, their weight a testament to the day's efforts. The walk back home is long and our footsteps are heavy, but there's a quiet pride in the air.

*

THAT EVENING, as we sit around the table, tired but content, a sharp knock breaks the calm. It's unusual for visitors to come unannounced, especially at this hour. My brother and I glance at each other, curiosity and unease passing between us. Mum pauses mid-step, her hand clutching the edge of her wrapper as she turns towards the door.

"I'll get it," I say quickly, pushing back my chair.

The wooden floorboards creak softly beneath my feet as I approach the door. The knock comes again, louder this time, echoing through the house. My hand hesitates on the latch, a faint nervousness curling in my chest.

When I open it, the sight before me takes my breath away. There is a tall woman with skin the colour of polished mahogany, radiating warmth and dignity. She's wearing an *Ankara* dress, blue and gold swirling in vibrant patterns that seem to come alive in the fading light. Her headwrap is perfectly tied, crowning her head with elegance, and from her ears dangle simple gold earrings that catch the last glints of sunlight, adding a soft glow to her face.

For a moment, I'm frozen, but then recognition hits like a wave. "Mama Esther!" I gasp, surprise and joy flooding my voice. She's Mummy's closest friend, almost like family. She'd visit us in Isumpe, bringing hot *akara* with sliced fresh chilli and onion inside—the best I've ever tasted. She sells them for a living. Memories are rushing back and I feel a sting behind my eyes, a swell of emotions I hadn't expected.

She smiles, and in a second, I'm wrapped in her arms. Her embrace is strong, warm, smelling of spices and a familiar softness that instantly pulls me back to Isumpe. It's a hug that says all the things words can't—that she's here, that she's missed us, that somehow, despite the distance, we're still connected.

"Look at you, all grown up," she says, her hands resting on my shoulders as she studies my face. Her eyes are damp, reflecting a mix of pride, sadness, and love. I blink, trying to keep my own tears at bay.

I invite Mama Esther inside, offering her a seat and a cup of tea. She settles, waiting for Mum to join us. "How is Mummy?" I ask, my voice barely above a whisper, afraid of the answer yet needing to hear it. A shadow crosses her face before she musters a small smile.

"Your mother is doing okay," she replies, attempting to infuse her words with cheerfulness. "You know how she is, tough as nails."

But her façade crumbles quickly as her eyes brim with tears, one escaping and trailing down her cheek. She wipes it away hastily, but not before I see the worry etched deep within her gaze. "She's been working hard, but times are tough," she continues, her voice cracking slightly. "She misses you both terribly." The weight of her words settles heavily in my chest, igniting a familiar ache of longing and guilt. I picture Mummy in Isumpe, her hands roughened by endless labour, her face lined with worry yet still radiating the gentle strength that has always been her hallmark.

As Mum joins Mama Esther in the parlour, the rest of us excuse ourselves, but I linger just outside, hiding in the shadows with my heart pounding. I wonder if she has news about Mummy. Good or bad, I brace myself, praying that the shadow is still kept at bay. I edge closer, straining to hear. This woman isn't known to anyone in my uncle's household except my brother and me, so the only reason she'd be here would have to be Mummy.

I watch her lips moving as they talk, but their words blur in my mind. They're chatting about everyday things: the neighbourhood, jobs, trivial updates. I wait, shifting on my feet, hoping Mummy's name will come up, wishing for reassurance that she's well.

Mama Esther compliments my uncle and aunt, commending them for their kindness in housing my brother and I, and providing an education. Mum, in her usual soft tone, replies, "What are family for?"

Then, the question I've been hoping for. My uncle's wife asks, "So, when did you last see the kids' mother?"

"Oh, not long ago," our visitor replies with a warm smile. "She's doing really great, actually."

My heart finally relaxes, relief washing over me as I slip away from the corner. Mummy is fine.

Sleep refuses to come. I lie in bed, staring at the ceiling or watching moonlight cast shadows that dance across the room. Thoughts of Mummy crowd my mind—her sacrifices, her struggles, the loneliness she must feel. I think of my performance in school, where I strive to come first or second in a class of fifty students. Every achievement is a step closer to my only dream: setting Mummy free from suffering.

ONE AFTERNOON, THE news I've longed for finally arrives. My uncle's wife declares over lunch, "We'll be visiting your mother this Christmas. It's been too long; I think you're both due for it."

My heart leaps. I race to my room and let out a muffled scream of joy into my pillow. Five years. It's been five years since we last saw her, and I can't wait to see her face, to feel her arms around me.

But as the days inch closer to our visit, a thought starts to grow. Just a hug and excitement won't be enough. Mummy has so little, and a simple visit feels incomplete without bringing something along. It's Christmas—a time for rice, tinned tomatoes, and all the little luxuries she can rarely afford. From memory, she usually buys these on credit and then works herself to the bone to repay it over the next few months. In my uncle's house, such things are plentiful, bought in sacks and cartons. I stand in the kitchen, staring at the two sacks of rice and the stacks of tinned tomatoes in the pantry. They're overflowing here, while Mummy would have none.

A plan begins to form, small and uncertain at first, but it grows with each passing day until it's all I can think about.

THE MORNING OF our departure dawns bright and crisp. After breakfast, while the others are busy with chores, I quietly slip into the pantry. The room is cool and dim, shelves lined with yams, beans, and a large sack resting in the corner. I glance over my shoulder, making sure I'm alone, then carefully open the sack. My hands shake as I pick up a generous amount of rice, filling a black plastic bag I have hidden in my apron pocket. Each scoop fills me with equal parts fear and excitement. The thought of Mummy cooking this rice, having a meal without the burden of debt, fills me with warmth.

I tuck the black bag deep into my cheap "Ghana Must Go" bag, the weight of it pressing against my side as we prepare for the trip. It's not much, but it feels monumental.

DOOM! DOOM! DOOM! My heart hammers in my chest as I sit wedged in the back of my uncle's Peugeot 505 wagon with five other children, all crammed together. My bag of stolen rice is hidden among the clothes in my bag at the back of the car. Up front, my uncle grips the wheel, navigating with practiced ease, while Mum

✱ THE GOOD THIEF

sits beside him. The journey is long, and as we near our village, the road grows wilder, tossing the car over deep, uneven potholes. A thick cloud of red dust kicks up, covering us, seeping through the windows. The smell of petrol fills the cramped space, making my stomach churn, but I don't mind. By the end of today, I'll finally be seeing Mummy, the woman who gave me life. And for the first time, she's going to eat without working herself to the bone. I can't wait to see the joy in her eyes when she receives my gift.

The excitement is tinged with a fear of getting caught. Thoughts keep clawing at my mind, but I push them aside. This small act of defiance is worth it for Mummy.

As the sun dips toward the horizon, we crawl closer to the village. The car groans, weary from the rough journey, just as our anticipation reaches its peak. Shadows stretch long across the road, and familiar sights emerge through the dust: trees, mud-brick houses, and people milling about, returning from the stream or the market. The village is alive with the hum of Christmas preparations—voices, laughter, the clink of pots. Villagers stop to watch us, some on foot, some on bicycles, curiosity flaring in their eyes. Cars are rare in Isumpe; no one here owns one, so our arrival is met with stares and murmurs.

"Is it Ifelunwa?" someone shouts, recognizing me. News spreads like fire through dry grass. Kids chase after us, waving and calling my name. My heart swells as I realise how much I have and how far I've come. Things I take for granted are precious here. The weight of gratitude settles over me, a reminder of all that I'm blessed with.

✱

FINALLY, WE PULL up in front of our old mud hut. Mummy is already there, alerted by the neighbours. She's standing with my younger siblings, her face lighting up with joy. Her cries of

PIECES OF ME ♥ JESSICA BAILEY

excitement echo through the air. The villagers buzz around us as the car doors open. I step down in my blue suit, polished shoes, and little hat, feeling like royalty. I imagine that I look like Queen Elizabeth.

Mummy rushes forward, tears streaming down her face. I can feel her love even before she reaches me. Bags are unloaded from the car, and my brother looks around, silent and wide-eyed, taking in this strange place, the unfamiliar faces, his own siblings whom he barely remembers. It's been so long that he's forgotten his roots.

As we settle in, Mummy brings out the small pot of *egusi* soup she'd carefully prepared, enough for just herself and my younger siblings. But now she offers it to us all, sacrificing her own meal with quiet grace. My uncle and his wife squeeze into our one-room mud hut, my brother lingering at the door. Back at my uncle's home, he and I have separate rooms. But here, Mummy and her children share this single space, its untarred floor and cracked walls. My brother seems bewildered, eyes darting around, unsure of where to sit. The only furniture is a long wooden bench, propped up by stones, where my uncle and his wife take their seats. Mummy hurries to borrow another bench from a neighbour so the others can sit, while my siblings and I settle on the mat, laughing and catching up.

Soon, there's a knock at the door, then another, and another. Word of our arrival has spread through the village, and friends I haven't seen in ages—Isioma, Nkechi, Charity—come by to say hello. We hand out biscuits, sharing small treats as memories flood back, each face a reminder of simpler times.

Later, as Mummy steps into the small kitchen, I follow her. Taking a deep breath, I tell her what I have in my bag. I say that I bought it with money I saved. Mummy was so proud. She hugs me, and I've never felt closer to her. For the first time, I've done something tangible to ease her burdens, to bridge the distance between us. My resolve to keep providing for her only deepens; I dream of a day when I can care for her fully, without limits.

*

THAT EVENING, MY uncle and his children leave, promising to return in a few days to take my brother and me back. Until then, these days with Mummy feel like a stolen treasure. I think that Christmas should last forever, with laughter, food, and the warmth of old friendships. My brother remains distant, a stranger in his own family. He tries to fit in, but the gap carved by years apart is a chasm too wide to cross in just a few days.

*

STEALING BECOMES ROUTINE. If I'm not the one taking rice or flour, it's outsiders like Mama Esther, or a kind neighbour who understands. I cling to the memory of Mummy's tears of joy the first time I brought her food, wanting to keep that feeling alive. It's easy to tell myself that it's simply my share, that what I take would have been mine anyway. The guilt lingers, but it's dulled by a sense of duty.

But secrets rarely stay hidden.

One evening, as the sun dips low and shadows stretch across the yard, my uncle calls me into the parlour. He sits on the worn-out sofa, his gaze cold and unwavering. Mum sits beside him, her hands clasped, her expression unreadable. "Come forward," he says.

I step closer, my heart pounding, palms slick with sweat. My mind races, searching for what might have triggered this ominous summons.

"The rice in the pantry has been disappearing unusually fast," he begins, his voice measured and sharp. "Do you have any idea why that might be happening?"

A chill runs down my spine, but I meet his gaze, hoping to mask my fear. "No," I answer, feigning innocence. "We've just been eating it."

But the weight of my deception presses down on me, and within moments, the truth unravels. My aunt's niece, who'd been visiting over the holidays and whom I once trusted to help, has betrayed me. My uncle and aunt's faces twist with anger and disappointment. My attempts to explain fall on deaf ears—they don't want to hear about the hunger, the need, or the love that drove me to it. In their eyes, a thief is a liar, and a liar is unforgivable.

"You're lucky you're in your final year of secondary school," my uncle says coldly. "Once you're done, you'll be out on the streets where you belong." His words cut deep, slicing through any lingering hope of understanding.

I try to make them see, to understand the desperation behind my actions, but their judgment is final. From that night on, I am a stranger in their home.

The warmth that once filled the household is replaced by a chilling distance. Conversations are curt, glances are filled with suspicion, and our once-harmonious routine becomes strained. Meals are eaten in silence, and I find myself alone more often than not.

I know my time here is up. Every tense moment and unkind glance tells me what words can't. Even my siblings sense the change, casting uncertain looks my way, unsure how to bridge the growing distance between us.

✳

ONE EVENING, I sit alone, tracing circles in the dirt by the doorway until I hear a faint whisper in the wind. It's a call to leave. To find somewhere I can start anew, redefine myself and my purpose. The thought fills me with both dread and a strange, liberating excitement.

I make the decision to leave before they can push me out. The journey will be mine to choose, the next steps mine to take. My resolve hardens, a spark lighting within.

The next morning, the house is peaceful. Uncle Patrick is at work, his wife is busy, and my cousins and brother are at school. I gather my things and slip away quietly, leaving behind a note which expresses my thanks for the shelter they gave me and understanding that my time with them has ended.

What lies ahead is unknown, but it can't be worse than the cold stares and bitter silence that surrounded me back there.

CHAPTER 7:
THE LONG ROAD

THE SUN DIPS low in the sky, casting an orange glow over the countryside. Dust billows up as we speed along the uneven road, heading towards Benin City. I don't know exactly where this rickety bus is taking me, but I do know it's pulling me further and further from everything I've ever known.

I've arranged to squat with Julie, an old high school mate, though it's funny because we were never close back then. Isn't it strange how desperation brings people together? She's in Benin with her older sister, who's living with her boyfriend. They've got a cramped little place, but said they'd make room for me until I can sort myself out. Julie reckons there's work I can find straight away, which means that I'll start getting paid soon. I don't have much choice.

The thought of getting a job before going to university doesn't sit right, but here I am. In another life, I would be sitting for the

Unified Tertiary Matriculation Exam, which is supposed to open doors to university and a life of stability and success. But no one thought to enrol me. No one seemed to care. The chaos, the shame, and the unspoken resentment have swallowed me whole, leaving little room for dreams. I'll have to work and save up if I ever want to take the exam. And with any luck, I might be able to keep a bit aside for Mummy too.

My chest tightens. Mummy has no idea where I am, or that I'm even on this bus. I've kept my plan quiet, partly because she'd never let me do it. She'd be devastated if she found out I'd been thrown out of Uncle Patrick's house. Phones have only just started becoming common across Nigeria, but in our village, they're rare—mostly owned by those with enough money to run a phone booth shop. Hiring a phone to call her would take her weeks of saving for just a few minutes of conversation. The thought of her scraping together coins to talk to me makes my stomach twist.

Mummy has always believed that education is our only hope. She's always dreamed that, one day, we'd go off to university, land good jobs, and escape our life of struggle. And now, here I am, abandoning that dream for the chance to scrape by on a stranger's floor.

The bus jerks suddenly as we hit a pothole, jolting me back to the present. Around me, people clutch their bags and mutter under their breath, but I barely notice them. I can't shake the feeling that this road might lead me somewhere I can't return from. But I don't have the luxury of second thoughts. I'm doing this for Mummy, for the chance to give her a better life and repay her for all the sacrifices she's made.

A memory drifts up, unbidden: a vision of Mummy's face the last time I saw her. She was laughing as she held out a bowl of *egusi* soup for us, giving us everything she had, even though it meant going hungry herself. I can't tell her. She'd insist I come back, beg my uncle for forgiveness. And that's something I can't do. I won't go back. Not to that cold house, not to the silence that's replaced any sense of belonging.

I glance around the bus, at the faces of the other passengers. Each one carries their own story. A woman holds a squirming toddler, while a young man stares intently at his hands, lost in thought. I wonder if they're as unsure of their futures as I am; if they too are running from something they can't bear to face.

As the bus rattles on, my thoughts turn to Julie. I can't quite picture what life with her will be like. In school, we only exchanged a few words. I was either the prefect or the assistant prefect in every class, which meant I mostly hung around with others who studied hard and did well. Julie wasn't in that category. Now, we're about to be thrown together in this strange twist of fate. There's a gnawing voice in the back of my mind, whispering doubts. What if this doesn't work out? What if I can't find a job? What if I'm just dragging myself deeper into a life I'll never escape? I push those thoughts away, clinging to the image of Mummy's smile, to the warmth I felt every time she looks at me with pride. I'm doing this for her. And maybe, in the process, I'll find a way to save myself, too.

As night falls, I wrap my arms around my bag, as if holding onto this one bit of security will somehow keep me safe. The bus rocks me into a restless sleep, and in my dreams, I see Mummy's worried eyes watching me as I walk further and further away. The road stretches on, and I don't look back.

BENIN CITY, WITH its crowded streets and endless noise, is nothing like home. I settle in with Julie, sharing a cramped one-room flat where every inch of space is accounted for. There's barely room to move, let alone breathe, but I'm grateful. She's given me a lifeline, and I can't afford to be picky.

In no time, Julie finds me a job right next to hers, working at a small photocopy shop that serves the university students. It's not glamorous. I'm surrounded by dusty shelves piled with paper, the noise of the copier and the constant clatter of students demanding prints for last-minute assignments. The pay isn't much, but it's enough to give to Mummy. I reconnect with her through one of her friends on Facebook. At first, she fretted constantly, imagining all the things that could go wrong. But as the days passed and she heard me forming a routine, she settled. I use a nearby phone booth to stay in touch with her, so she knows not to worry about me. I send her money at the end of each month to keep her fed and give her a taste of comfort.

Still, seeing those students' day after day—laughing and studying, with their eyes bright and minds full of possibilities—feels like salt on a wound. Each passing face reminds me of the life I was meant to have and the dreams I've tucked away in a dark corner, waiting for a time when I can afford them. Here they are, living that life, while I'm on the outside looking in. I tell myself it's worth it, but the ache gnaws at me like a slow-burning fire.

∗

My life becomes predictable. Work. Earn. Send money. Day after day, it's the same grind, the same sacrifice. It's for Mummy, I keep reminding myself. It's for Mummy.

∗

Then my sister calls. Her voice is low, filled with an urgency I've never heard before. "Mummy's not well," she says, and I feel my heart stop. I don't even need to ask what's wrong. It's her heart problem, the one we've all pretended wasn't creeping up on her. But now it's caught her, and she's slipping away.

I feel my hands go cold. Mummy. The thought of her being frail and struggling to breathe cuts through me like a knife. We all knew this day would come, but I never thought it would be now. What if she doesn't make it?

The salary I earn is barely enough to feed Mummy and my younger siblings, let alone pay for hospital bills. I sit in the corner of our cramped room that night, my mind racing and my heart pounding with the helplessness of it all. I need money. Real money. Not the pitiful wage I'm earning here, but something that will actually make a difference.

Desperation claws at me, whispering ideas I'd never considered before. A shortcut to make things right. Marry a rich man, perhaps. Find someone who could make this nightmare go away. Or something worse, something that makes my skin crawl just thinking about it. Use myself, trade my dignity, sacrifice my soul if I have to. Anything to keep Mummy safe. I don't want Death in our house. I don't want it to take Mummy the way it took Father. I can feel it here knocking, its fingers gripping our door. I need to do something. If Mummy dies, my siblings will expect me to look at her, to face her body. But I can't. I can't look at bodies. May God forbid it, that day must never come.

These thoughts are a dark stain on my mind, impossible to scrub clean. No matter how I try to distract myself, Death lurks, reminding me of everything I can't escape. I close my eyes, and there's Mummy—her worn-out face, her thin smile, the way she'd always say, "Everything will be alright." Now it's me who has to reassure her.

In Julie's cramped room, surrounded by flaking paint and the smell of damp clothes, I make a silent promise, my fists clenched until my nails bite into my palms. I'll do whatever it takes. No matter what it costs me.

Days pass in a blur of photocopied pages and fleeting moments. I can feel time running out. Then a man appears. Lucas is miner from Australia, twice my age with a rough voice and a wallet thick with promise. He doesn't offer love; he offers escape. He says he can keep Mummy safe. And so, standing in a dimly-lit bar, I am twenty years old with my heart numb and mind resolute. I whisper, "Yes, I do."

After the wedding, things change. The money flows. Mummy no longer limits her cups of tea or hesitates to buy bread. She tells me she feels stronger, that her heart isn't as heavy.

Lucas yells at me until the walls shake, his towering figure casting shadows that swallow the light.

CHAPTER 8:
LA-LA LAND

AS LUCAS AND I step out of the airport in Perth, Western Australia, a chill breeze hits my face. We've just arrived from Africa, and everything here already feels like a different world. Standing in the glow of the airport lights is an elderly White man, maybe in his eighties, with silver hair, a tall frame, and a face deeply lined but full of warmth. He smiles at us with an ease that I find comforting but strange.

"Hi, Dad," Lucas says, walking up to him. There's so much respect in his voice, almost reverence. Lucas's dad nods and pats his shoulder, then reaches for our bags, lifting them with surprising strength for someone his age. I'm caught off guard, watching him handle the weight as if he's done it every day of his life. Where I come from, a man his age would be seen as fragile, not someone who lifts luggage and drives at night. This kind of energy and strength should be unimaginable.

The elderly man leads us to his gleaming green Mitsubishi. Lucas takes the passenger seat, leaving his dad to drive. I slide into the back, wondering how someone his age is still behind the wheel. As we pull out of the car park, he handles the vehicle with a smoothness that only comes from years of experience. He's chatting with Lucas, his voice calm, even a bit lively, and I can't stop staring. A man in his eighties, alive, strong, and alert—it seems impossible, like a glimpse into some sort of fantasy land. I wonder, is this the place where there is no Death?

The drive takes less than thirty minutes, but I'm captivated by every second of it. Outside the window, the streets are quiet and orderly, illuminated by rows of streetlights that glow without flickering, steady and reliable. The lawns are all trimmed perfectly, each blade of grass neatly in place. Trees stand tall and proud along the road, their branches swaying softly in the night breeze, and the air smells fresh, clean. Even the sky seems different; vast and open, a deep, endless blue.

WE PULL INTO a driveway. Waiting at the door of a house are two young White children and an elderly White woman with a soft, gentle face. Memories of Uncle Patrick's kids racing towards him on the day I arrived at his house are rushing back to me—only this time, just over a year after I left there, I'm seeing the faces of my stepchildren. I'm only 22, but this is now my reality. The kids run to Lucas, laughing as they jump into his arms. He hugs them tightly, and walks over to the soft-faced woman, wrapping her in an embrace.

"Hi, Mum," he says softly, leaning in for a quick kiss.

I blink, almost in disbelief. "Hi, Mum?" This woman is his mother? She's alive, too? I can hardly process it. In my village, Death hovers constantly, snatching away mothers and fathers, leaving children to grow up too fast, forcing them to learn survival before they've even understood childhood. But here, Lucas has both his parents alive, healthy and strong. What kind of place is this?

But this new freedom has its own snags, starting from the very first meal. Their family dining table is set with pristine silverware that glints under soft, golden light. I sit beside Lucas and his two young children as his mother, Anne, serves dinner. She places plates in front of us, filled with dishes I've never seen before: leafy greens that look like something picked straight from the garden, and a slab of steak that oozes red in the middle, the sight of it making my stomach churn. Lucas and the kids pick up their knives and forks, slicing through the meat with the ease of years of practice, eating with a quiet grace.

I grip my own fork and knife, clumsy in my hands, trying to mimic their movements. Anne catches my eye and smiles, her gaze warm and welcoming, but there's a tightness in my throat. I feel like an intruder in this pristine world, like a stranger trying to fit into a place where I don't quite belong. I want to tell myself it's only temporary, that I'll adjust, that I'll make it work. I have to. After all, Lucas is providing for my family, sending money back home to keep Mummy and my siblings afloat. This is what I came for.

AS DAYS PASS, I take in the immaculate lawns, the perfectly pruned bushes, the tall trees lining the street like guardians of some hidden paradise. Back home, power outages are common; darkness comes without warning, as does grief. Here, the lights shine bright and steady, the houses stand firm, and everything seems built to last.

A warmth spreads through me, an unfamiliar feeling that I can only describe as hope. Maybe, just maybe, I've escaped. Maybe I've left the shadows behind, crossed some invisible line that Death can't follow. Here, in this land where gardens are perfect and parents grow old, I feel a strange sense of peace. If I could show my family this life, that would be a dream worth holding on to.

I imagine Mummy here, walking these spotless streets, her face free of the constant worry that shadows her back home. No more wails in the night, no more endless mourning, no more fear. Here, she could know happiness without the dark edges and lurking dread. She'd have to adjust to some things—the strange foods, the new routines—but that seems like a small price to pay for a life free of loss and fear.

This place is perfect. The air, the sky, the streetlights that never flicker. Everything feels permanent, untouched by decay. For the first time, I let myself believe that maybe I've truly left the monsters behind.

Back home, it is rare to see grandchildren. Here in Australia, people don't die. I no longer hear the loud cries of people, mourning loved ones. It used to be hard to think of anything else. Here, all that is over. Lucas is taking care of my family's needs for now, sending money back home to them. He yells at me sometimes, but for the role he plays in my family, it's a price worth paying.

*

But reality soon rears its head. There's an unspoken cost, one that tugs at me every day, reminding me that nothing in this world comes without a price. Every time I call home and hear Mummy's voice, the distance feels vast, like we're on separate planets. Her gratitude for the money I send reminds me that my sacrifices are not in vain. But there's no end date to this journey, no finish line. I sit alone in my room, my heart aching, realising all I've given up: my youth, my education, the warmth of Mummy's home. All of it, now just memories.

And yet, amid the sorrow, there's solace. Writing is my one escape, the only thing that makes me feel alive. Lucas lets me borrow his computer, and as my fingers move across the keyboard,

I feel a thrill seeing my words appear on the screen, polished and crisp. Back home, I could only dream of using a computer. I scribbled stories in an old exercise book. But here, I write freely, and sometimes Lucas prints out my pages. Holding my words on paper, I feel a surge of hope. Maybe one day, someone will hold my book in their hands and read my story.

*

I SIT IN a career adviser's office, watching as he scrolls through pages on his laptop, his face serious. "This is where people like you thrive," he says, pointing to a list of jobs in nursing, aged care and support work. His voice is firm, as if he's stating a fact of life. I swallow hard, a bitter taste filling my mouth. In their eyes, I'm African, I'm Black, and I'm only fit for caring for others, never creating. My passion and my voice are unwelcome here.

I can't keep going like this, living a life that feels like a shadow of who I am. But the thought of going back terrifies me more than anything. Staying here keeps the shadows far, far away, and staying with nursing promises hope for my family.

So, I sign up. I wear the scrubs, tie on the baggy pants that feel like a prison uniform. Each day, I walk into classes where words like "syringe" and "antiseptic" sound foreign and cold. Lunch is my lifeline. It's the only time I can breathe, tell stories and feel a little of the person I used to be. My classmates notice, too. "You're a natural storyteller," they tell me. "You should really pursue it." I chuckle hollowly because I've heard it all before. My friends back home used to say the same thing, and now, halfway across the world, I hear it again, like an echo of a life I can't return to.

CHAPTER 9:
BAD PEOPLE

I'M HALFWAY THROUGH my practicum at a St John of God hospital, part of the clinical requirements for my course. I stand in the hallway, eyes glued to the clock on the opposite wall, willing the minute hand to inch forward.

Footsteps and chatter echo down the corridor. A group of my fellow students walks past, all of them dressed in identical scrubs and wearing smiles that I can't relate to. They look excited, buzzing with energy that feels entirely out of place in this sterile, fluorescent-lit hall.

I step forward and catch one of them by the arm. "Where are you all headed?"

"To the morgue!" she says, grinning. Her eyes are alight, as if this is some kind of thrill at a theme park.

I blink, certain I've misheard. "The what?"

"The morgue," she repeats, still smiling. "We're going to see a body. Dead people."

Her words are sharp and cold. I release her arm and she joins the others, their laughter trailing down the hall as they disappear around the corner. I watch them fade away, my chest tight and my throat dry.

Images I've worked so hard to bury flash before my eyes. Screams and wails. The thud of shovels against dirt. The smell of earth and rot, mingled with something else, something I can't name and can't forget. It clings to memories I tried to leave far behind.

My legs feel like lead as I walk out of the hospital. Outside, the cold air hits my face, and I gasp, desperate for breath that doesn't seem to come. And then, without looking back, I leave.

A part of me shatters; knowing I've abandoned the only path that promised hope for my family, the dream of finishing school, of being financially free. It feels like failure, like a closed door to freedom.

Every time I choose a new way to avoid Death, it finds its own ways to catch up with me. It appears in every angle, in every shadow, seeping into the lives around me. Uncle Ifeanyi, gone. Brother Opi, gone. Almost all of the people I used to know have been taken. Each loss drives me deeper into hiding, and I make a pact with myself to keep Death at a distance. If I don't see it, it doesn't exist.

Then Death takes Uncle Patrick. My brother calls from across the ocean, spilling details of the family gathering; the funeral, the burial. His words pull me closer to the reality I keep trying to ignore. I want him to stop, but I also need to hear it.

Uncle Patrick's face haunts my dreams. I have memories so vivid that they seem to defy the miles that separate us. He wasn't perfect, but he's the only father figure that my brother and I can remember. I planned to reconnect with him, to reach out and say thank you again, without the bitterness. I did try; I called him once from Australia, but I didn't have the courage to speak, and he didn't know who was calling him by the phone number alone. He never knew that I wanted to thank him, and now I can't have more time with him to say it.

Piece by piece, I shut down. I tell myself it's easier to let numbness settle, to let my world grow smaller, colder. Denial will protect me.

But then there's another call. My godmother is gone now, too.

My mind spirals. Ifeanyi. Opi. Daddy. And my godmother. Death is no longer a visitor in my life; it's a resident, lurking in my home. Someone is letting it in.

I want to believe it's all in my mind, but then the whispers start. My brother tells me stories of our old neighbours killing people. I dream of deals with Death, trading one life for another.

Maybe the aunties know something. The way they would glance and murmur behind my back made me wonder what they were saying. Could it be about me? My family? What if Mummy actually did kill Father? I can't ignore the nightmares anymore; the ones where she chases me relentlessly with a cutlass. What if my dreams aren't just dreams? What if my mind is warning me?

I feel a shiver. What if it wasn't Mummy? What if Grandpa was the killer? Could he have killed his own sons, our greatest hopes, to add more years to his old age? He's still alive now. It feels too convenient, too strange to me that he's outlived all his siblings, and now he's outliving all his children. Will he put my brother in danger next? Am I in danger too?

PIECES OF ME ♥ JESSICA BAILEY

I want to scream, to run, but where can I go? I'm trapped by the people I should feel safest with. The walls feel like they're closing in. I can't escape forever. I know that. But I don't know who to trust. My own family, the ones I love, have become the ones I fear the most.

I lie awake at night, eyes wide open, feeling Death's shadow in my room. I distance myself, cut off ties, sever connections until the only ones left in my world are the people under my roof: my children and my husband. My small family here in Australia are the only people I hold close.

✼

But even that safety is an illusion. The numbness I clung to shatters. Change starts with words spat in anger, then fists slamming on tables, objects raised. The man I trusted, who swore to protect me, becomes someone to fear. Every day, I feel myself shrinking, folding inward, trying to disappear. I can't escape the feeling that my time is ticking down. I know what I have to do.

Over the last ten years, I fought racism, battled discrimination, and endured domestic violence. I was pushed down, silenced, and made to feel very small, right up until the moment I stood up as tall as I truly am, and said to them all, "*No more.*"

My life starts to take shape in ways I once thought impossible. My passion—once buried under survival—is finding its way into the light. I'm standing on my own two feet in Australia, no longer just existing, but building something real. I'm a young African-Australian woman with a degree in filmmaking and journalism, an industry-funded short film titled *I'm Not a Nurse* on the way, and the seed of a book stirring restlessly inside me, waiting to be born. I feel the urgency and importance of it all in my bones: these dreams matter. There is so much at stake right now, and I feel the current of something even bigger pulling me forward. For the first time, I know I have something to give to Australia, and I'm the only one who can do it.

The creative dam inside me has burst open. Ideas flood in from every corner, visions for what I can create, who I can become, and how far I can go. And for the first time, I can finally see a future for myself which is filled to the brim with possibility. I am alive with excitement.

Lucas is blocked, my family is blocked, even Mummy is blocked. So now, it's just me and my children—the only family I can fully trust. Every possible threat has been sealed off and silenced. They carry old wounds, old chains, old shadows but most of all, they carry death. I can't let that happen to me. I can't give them any more chances; I can't risk any weakness in the walls I've built. Not now. I've cut them all off, like dead branches from a tree.

CHAPTER 10:
THE PHONE CALL

LATE AFTERNOON BATHES the basketball court in a golden glow as the game reaches its climax. Parents along the sidelines hold their breath, eyes glued to the court. In the midst of it all, M darts across the court, a basketball bouncing rhythmically under his control. His small frame is a blur of motion, fuelled by energy and determination. His curly afro bounces, catching the light as he dribbles with the confidence of someone much older.

"Go, M! Go on, hit it!" I shout, my voice blending with the cheers of the other parents. The excitement is contagious. My boy, El, along with the rest of *The Legend* team, are jumping around on the sidelines, unable to contain their enthusiasm.

"Go on, baby, show them what you've got!" I urge, my heart swelling with pride. M's tiny legs move with the speed and agility that only a seven-year-old could muster. He weaves through the opposition, showing his father's athleticism and my determination. His eyes are laser-focused, his movements calculated. The hours of training, the countless drills, the endless practice sessions—all of it is paying off right now. M powers forward, stretching his muscles. In one swift, practiced motion, he sends the ball soaring toward the hoop. It swishes through, clean and perfect.

The court erupts in cheers. We clap and shout, our voices mingling in a joyful chorus. M turns to look at me, his eyes bright with pride, his chest puffed out. His dream is to play for the NBA, and in this moment, I believe with all my heart that he can do it.

✻

As we walk back to the car park, the buzz of the game still lingers in the air. Other parents, some familiar faces and others new, offer words of encouragement as they pass by. A tall man with a warm smile stops me. "Your boy is good," he says, nodding toward M. "He'll go places."

I smile, a deep sense of pride welling up inside me. "Thank you," I reply. This is far from the first time we've heard such compliments, but it never gets old. Every kind word is another validation, another push to keep going.

M sits in the backseat, his eyes shining with excitement. "Mum, I really want to play for the NBA, like Kobe Bryant," he declares, his voice bubbling over with enthusiasm. His grin is so wide, it seems to light up the entire car. It's the unshakable confidence of a boy who believes, without a shadow of a doubt, that the world is his for the taking.

"The sky is your limit, baby," I say, my voice soft but confident, catching M's gaze through the rearview mirror. There's no stopping him. His dreams are vast, stretching far beyond our little world, and his determination is even bigger. I keep my eyes

* THE PHONE CALL

on him as he goes on and on about how he can't wait to turn eighteen and move to the US to start chasing his dreams. His voice is full of wonder, painting a picture of a future so bright it almost hurts to look at it.

Tears well up in my eyes, blurring the road ahead. It's been three years since the separation from their father. The boys and I have come a long way since then. A profound calm has settled over us, like we've stepped into someone else's life, where peace isn't something we have to fight for every day. Our mornings arrive like gentle waves, washing over us, smoothing the jagged edges of the past. And for the first time, I am not just surviving. I am living.

I have become a certified life coach and a speaker, using my voice to help others discover their hidden gifts and life's purpose. My journey here in Australia has given me an abundance of stories and hard-won wisdom, and all of it is moving me forward into a life I am proud of.

My first film, *I'm Not a Nurse*—written, directed, and brought to life by me—is no longer just a dream. It is out in the world, earning nominations and winning awards across the globe. The book by the same name is also finding its way into hearts, resonating with those who read it. And this is only the beginning. There are more films stirring within me, ready to rise. This is a life—my life—where the future is full of possibilities.

We walk into the house, and the boys' laughter fills the air, a sound so pure and joyous it's like birdsong at dawn. Their voices, excited and unrestrained, echo through the rooms, filling every corner with happiness. M, who is 7, El, who is 11, and their half-brother E, at 16 (whom I did not give birth to, yet he has chosen to live with me) are moving through the house like sunbeams, their energy illuminating everything in their path. They're growing so fast—too fast—but their innocence remains untouched.

PIECES OF ME ♥ JESSICA BAILEY

✱

FAMILY TIES, ONCE strained and frayed, are mended and stronger than ever. Anne and Gordon, their grandparents, have become like parents to the boys and me, and the best memories of Christmases and birthdays are created at their home. Anne, always the heart of our gatherings, bakes cakes for birthdays, and we show up just to nibble at them, basking in her love. But age begins to tell on them, so my boys and I have started to take on more responsibilities.

For Gordon's 96th birthday, the kids made their first attempt at a vanilla cake. The candles, shaped like a 9 and a 6, are arranged meticulously on the cake. El's concentration is so intense, it's as if he's building something sacred. E, ever the prankster, catches El's eye, and with a quick twist of his hand, he flips the 9 upside down, turning it into a 6. They both laugh quietly, sharing a moment of brotherly mischief.

The candles are corrected and lit, their tiny flames flickering in the gentle breeze that drifts through the room. I glance over at Gordon, lying peacefully in his bed. The man who once towered over us now seems so small, his body frail, his energy subdued. His eyes are clouded with age but still hold a glimmer of the man who taught me how to drive and was once the pillar of our family.

The urge to capture this moment overwhelms me. I reach for my phone, my hands trembling slightly. "Go on, get in the frame, all of you," I say, my voice barely above a whisper but filled with urgency. M, El, and E gather around Gordon's bed, their faces glowing with the pure, unfiltered joy of children. Anne, sits beside them, her smile soft but weary, the weight of her responsibilities etched into her features.

The camera clicks, freezing this moment in time, leaving me with a bittersweet realisation that these days are numbered. As the

* THE PHONE CALL

image forms on the screen, I feel a pang of sadness mixed with gratitude.

Later, as we drive home, E is at the wheel. His posture is relaxed, his hands steady. I watch him, a mix of pride and trepidation filling my heart. It's hard to believe that the boy who once needed help to tie his shoes is now a young man, navigating the world with his own sense of purpose.

From the back seat, M pipes up, his voice filled with envy. "E's so lucky, he's going to be drinking very soon cause he's turning eighteen."

"Yeah, and then he's going to finish high school," El adds, his voice tinged with a hint of awe. It's exciting and terrifying all at once, watching them grow and step into their own power.

At home, we unpack the food from Anne—pies, cakes, and curry stew—reminding me how much she has supported us since I started university.

AND THEN THERE'S Martin.

He enters my life quietly, like the soft rustling of leaves on a summer evening. The first time our eyes meet, it's as if the universe has shifted, aligning us in a way that feels both primal and inevitable. There's an intensity in his gaze that draws me in like a moth to a flame.

Martin is solid, like the earth beneath my feet, grounding and comforting in ways I never knew I needed. His touch is like cool linen against sun-kissed skin, a gentle caress that lingers long after he's gone. Our love grows not in grand gestures, but in the quiet spaces between moments. It's in the silences that we share, where words would only diminish the depth of our connection. It's in the laughter that flows easily between us, as natural as breathing, as if we've known each other for lifetimes.

With Martin by my side, the world tilts in my favour. My second book, *The One,* was inspired by the love we share, its pages filled with the passion and creativity he brings out in me. It's not just a dream realised; it's proof that the universe is listening, aligning itself with our desires. The doors that once felt firmly shut now stand wide open, and I walk through them with a confidence I've never known. My voice grows stronger, my network expands, and my profile rises like the sun after a long, dark night. The energy within me is boundless, a tidal wave of ambition and creativity that propels me forward, unstoppable.

*

ONE EVENING, AS we walk hand-in-hand, I feel the universe whispering to me, urging me toward something greater. The stars above seem to pulse with a rhythm that matches the beating of my heart, each one a tiny beacon of possibility. I turn to Martin, his face illuminated by the soft glow of the moon, and the words tumble out of me, unbidden. "I want to go back to university and start a PhD," I say. My voice is steady and sure, the conviction in my words surprising even me.

Martin squeezes my hand, his grip warm and reassuring. He turns to me, his eyes sparkling with a mixture of amusement and pride. "Give me three reasons," he says, his voice a low rumble, teasing yet earnest.

I smile, my heart swelling with the love that overflows between us. The reasons pour out of me, each one a testament to the life we are building together. We have only just met, but things are moving quickly—perhaps too quickly. Martin introduces me to his mother, his sister, and his older son, and I feel a pang of guilt that I haven't even thought about when or how he will meet my kids, let alone my ex-in-laws. Anne has become like a mother to me, and the thought of breaking the news of my relationship to her is unimaginable. Yet every sign points to Martin being here for the long run.

*

As we sit under the shade in his backyard, sharing a cigar next to the pool, I voice what's been sitting on the edge of my thoughts. "I'm thinking that next Christmas is an ideal time to introduce you to the kids," I say, the statement hanging somewhere between a question and a declaration.

An uncomfortable silence stretches between us as I wait for Martin's response. He takes a drag from the cigar, smoke curling into the air before he exhales slowly. "We might be married by Christmas," he says with quiet confidence, and my heart flips. I wonder whether the kids will like him and whether he will like them.

The next day, as M and El open their Easter eggs, I pull Anne aside into her bedroom. There's a look of worry in her eyes as she asks, "What is it, love?"

"I met someone," I blurt out.

Anne sits in silence for a moment, her expression unreadable. Then she gives me a hug, and as she pulls back, there's a softness in her eyes that makes tears well up in mine. "I expected that you would move on one day," she says. "It's okay. That doesn't change my love for you."

The following day, with that same momentum, I gather the boys in a quiet room. "I met someone," I tell them, my heart pounding in my chest.

Their eyes widen, a mix of surprise and curiosity playing across their faces. Then the questions come in a rush. "What's he like? Are you going to marry him? When can we meet him?" My nightmare is over. It's such a relief. What freedom, to have it all out in the open.

A few weeks later, the kids and I are on a ferry ride to Rottnest Island with Martin. We're going to meet his mum, his sister, and her husband so we can celebrate his mum's birthday together.

The salty breeze hits my face, sunlight sparkles across the water, and the gentle rocking of the boat makes everything feel dreamlike. I can't quite believe this is real. After the separation from Lucas, I never imagined having a partner here in Australia who is loving and genuinely present for me and for my children. Watching Martin carry the bags, hold my hand, and guide the kids across the deck, I feel a deep sense of gratitude and wonder. It's a glimpse of what I never thought I could have: love, connection, and joy that includes all of us.

The kids feed white cockatoos with Linda, Martin's sister, and I'm amazed at how quickly they seem to bond. It's as if they've known each other for ages. The day is filled with laughter, food, and a few complaints about the long walks, but it's all perfect in its own way.

One morning, a text from Martin pops up on my phone, suggesting that I meet the last person remaining in his family: Dylan, his 16-year-old son. Though I'm eager to meet him, Martin is suggesting we do it the night before he leaves for his trip to the US. I hesitate. "You're only away for two weeks, no point rushing. We'll do it when you come back," I say.

But Martin insists, "Let's just get it out of the way," he says in his usual straightforward manner. Since we met, we've been getting a lot of things out of the way.

*

ON THE DAY I'm to meet Dylan, nothing in my wardrobe seems right. I do public speaking, so meeting people is usually second nature to me, but for some reason, I find myself trying on outfit after outfit, sweating as if I've been invited to a palace. I finally settle on something, when as there's nothing else to try.

Then I meet Dylan, and I understand. His beauty is undeniable, a striking mix of youthful confidence and something more reserved, more introspective.

"You are so beautiful," I tell him as he fastens his seatbelt in the back of the car, behind his father. He has a small, shy smile that tugs at my heart. "You should be on TV," I add as the car starts moving. Every word I speak to Dylan comes from the heart. He is a beautiful boy, inside and out, with a face I know I'll never forget.

At an Indian restaurant, we sit with two large pizzas in front of us. I sit directly opposite Dylan as he enjoys his Margherita pizza, his focus intense as he savours each bite.

"You should come with me to the US," Martin suggests lovingly.

"Nah, that's not me," Dylan replies, his voice steady and sure.

I smile, appreciating the honesty. I respect that. Throughout the evening, I can't stop marvelling at Dylan's beauty and quiet strength.

As we pull into the driveway, the tires crunch softly on the gravel and Dylan unbuckles his seatbelt with practiced ease, the click of the metal buckle echoing in the quiet night. He steps out of the car with a graceful confidence, the kind that comes from being comfortable in one's own skin. Martin follows, and they stand together for a moment—father and son—sharing a quiet conversation under the soft porch light. There's something tender in the way they interact, a bond of unspoken love and mutual respect.

Dylan turns towards me, his smile a reflection of the kindness that seems to radiate from him. "It was nice meeting you," he says, his voice carrying a sincerity that touches my heart.

I hesitate, the words catching in my throat before I find my voice. "Can I have a hug?" I ask, the question hanging in the air between us.

For a moment, time seems to pause. Dylan looks at me, his expression thoughtful, as if he's weighing the moment in his mind. Then, with a smile that reaches his eyes, he steps forward. We embrace, a shared connection that feels both new and familiar. His arms are strong yet gentle, and I can feel the warmth of his spirit, the kindness that seems to flow from him effortlessly.

Martin watches us, a soft smile playing on his lips as we break apart. Dylan heads towards the house, his footsteps light on the gravel, the sound fading as he disappears into the entryway. Martin takes his place behind the wheel, and as we drive away, I search for the words to express what I'm feeling. "You should be proud, your son is so beautiful," I say, my voice full of emotion.

Martin glances at me, his smile widening, a look of quiet pride in his eyes. "I know," he says simply, his tone filled with a father's love and gratitude.

A wave of emotion washes over me—envy, admiration, and something deeper, something more profound. I realise with a start that being Martin's partner also means being a part of Dylan's life. In that moment, I feel incredibly lucky, blessed to be in this position, to share in the love that binds this family together.

*

That night, Martin and I settle into our usual spot in the backyard, the warm breeze carrying the scent of blooming jasmine. We light cigars, the orange glow of the tips flaring briefly before settling into a steady burn, each puff a silent exhalation of gratitude for this shared moment of peace and contentment. We sit there, side by side, the night wrapping around us like a comforting blanket, our hearts full and our spirits high.

There's a sense of completeness between us, a quiet acknowledgment that we've crossed a threshold. We've met the people who matter most in each other's lives, and with that, there's a sense of release from any lingering doubts or fears. We owe nothing to anyone now—only to each other, and to the love that has grown between us.

As we sit there, our hands occasionally brushing together, Martin says, "I'm in a really good place right now."

"Me too," I respond. Martin leaves for the US soon, and the only shadow on our horizon is the thought of being apart. But even that seems insignificant in the grand scheme of things. Life is good. It feels like a dream—one of those perfect, sun-drenched dreams I never want to wake from.

His whispers of love in my ear are like the soundtrack to a movie. Even when he's thousands of miles away, flowers arrive at my door, tangible reminders of his affection, his presence felt even in his absence.

Everything is perfect.

*

It's a phone call that shatters the illusion, sending my heart racing in a way it hasn't in years. It comes after midnight, in the kind of deep, enveloping darkness that swallows everything in its path. My room is bathed in shadows, heavy curtains blocking out even the faintest glimmer of moonlight. The only light comes from the faint, pulsating glow of my cell phone vibrating on the nightstand. The screen flickers with life, casting an eerie blue light across the walls.

Martin's name flashes on the screen like a ghost from another world. The sight usually brings a smile to my face and a flutter of warmth in my chest. We spoke just before I went to bed, our voices full of love and longing as we counted down the hours until his return to Perth: forty-eight hours, 2,880 minutes, an eternity condensed into a moment. We laughed and I imagined our reunion, the feel of his arms around me, the sound of his heartbeat beneath my ear. But this time, something is wrong. My heart thuds, each beat a slow, ominous drumbeat that drowns out the stillness of the night. Martin knows the time difference between Australia and the US too well. He knows I would be sound asleep at 11pm. So why is he calling now?

I fumble with the phone, my fingers clumsy and shaking, as if the fear seeping through my veins has made them numb. The screen slips slightly under my sweaty fingertips, and I nearly drop it. My mind is racing, hurtling through a thousand scenarios, each one worse than the last. My breath catches in my throat as I finally press the green button. The sound of the call connecting is loud in the silence.

The voice that greets me is not the strong, confident man who has captured my heart. This voice is broken, trembling with a sorrow so deep it seeps through the line, making my blood run cold.

"Martin?" I whisper, my voice barely audible, quivering with the fear I can no longer hold back. "What's wrong?"

For a moment, there is nothing but the sound of his sobs, raw and unrestrained, echoing in the stillness of the night. Cold dread pools in the pit of my stomach. What could have happened? My mind spins, grasping at straws, trying to put together puzzle pieces that refuse to fit.

"Accident . . . " he finally chokes out, the word hanging in the air like a guillotine, poised to drop.

"Accident?" I echo, my voice no more than a shaky whisper, barely believing the word that now seems to vibrate in the air between us. "What kind of accident? Are you okay? Was it on the way to the airport?"

Panic surges through me, my thoughts spiralling out of control, each one more terrifying than the last. I see it all in my mind's eye: the twisted wreckage of a car, shattered glass glittering like diamonds in the night, the metallic smell of blood and gasoline and the wail of distant sirens. "Is it your leg? Are you hurt? Is it your mother?" I blurt out, desperation clawing at my throat, the words tumbling out in a frantic rush.

But Martin's sobs only grow louder, each one tearing through me like a jagged knife, his words tangled and choked by grief. When he finally speaks, his voice is so full of pain it makes my chest ache.

"It's Dylan." His words hit me like a punch to the gut. "My beautiful boy is gone. My beautiful boy. He never hurt anyone."

The room around me begins to spin, the walls closing in as if the world itself is collapsing under the weight of his words. Oh my God. Death has been lurking in the shadows, biding its time, and now it has found me. This is the darkness I've fought so hard to escape, the darkness that has haunted my every step, that has chased me halfway across the world.

I've been running for so long. But I can't run anymore, not this time, with its grip tightening on my throat and its sharp nails digging into my flesh. I realise there's nowhere left to run.

CHAPTER 11:
WE ARE FOOLS

WORDS REVERBERATE IN my mind, echoing in a space that was, just moments ago, occupied by the mundane worries of a keynote speech I was supposed to deliver today. My heart pounds, each beat a hammer driving the reality of Martin's world deeper into my consciousness. His son is gone. A boy I had pizza with just a couple of weeks ago, whose laughter still lingers in the corners of my mind.

I sit down on a park bench, the sunlight filtering through the trees above me, casting shifting patterns on the ground. The light feels harsh, as though it's highlighting the sharp edges of the news I've just received. My mind races, trying to unpack the magnitude of what Martin has just told me. The boy in question isn't just anyone—he's Martin's son. Martin is my partner, which makes Dylan . . . what? My stepson, if we were married? How close am I supposed to be to this pain?

We've only just started this relationship. We're still learning each other's quirks, still figuring out how we fit into each other's lives. Is it selfish to hope that I can stay on the sidelines, to support Martin without getting too close to this? There's going to be a body somewhere, and then a coffin, and a burial. I can't face this. What should I do?

My phone buzzes. It's a text from Martin.

I want you to come with me to see Dyl so that I can see you and have you to hold.

My heart sinks. The fear I've been holding at bay surges forward. I'm not just a bystander in this; Martin needs me by his side. The walls I've been trying to build crumble, along with my illusion of distance. The shift is dizzying, disorienting. It happened so fast. I didn't know it could occur in this manner. When Father died, it was a long illness that slowly crushed him. We saw him leaving. Right before we moved to Lagos, my younger brother Charles died, but we knew he was sick. We were warned.

The phone buzzes again—this time, it's a friend. I texted her about the news earlier on, and now she's calling, her voice a lifeline in the tumultuous sea of my thoughts.

"Jess, I am so sorry!" Bec says, her voice soft and full of empathy. Her words wash over me, and the gravity of what's happened begins to sink in. I can't hold it together anymore. The tears come, hot and unrelenting. I don't know what I am crying for, whether it's the fear of having to be in this situation, or out of empathy for the man I've just fallen in love with. Perhaps I feel pity for myself, for this ill luck that faces me. Why me, of all the people in the world? Why now?

My tears run for the little girl inside me who has carried her fear for so long and now is about to face it, and for the woman who is just beginning to open her heart again, only to have it tested by a tragedy she never saw coming. For all of the loved ones that passed over the years when I never got the chance to say goodbye or grieve them. The pain comes raw and sharp. I'm alone here, right now—this is my grief. Mummy isn't here to save me, Father isn't here, and there's no aunties, no uncles, no husband either. I am about to face my biggest fear and there is no one to protect me. I feel that I am both a child and an adult in this darkness, and somehow I must go through it.

"I don't know how to support him," I admit, my voice cracking under the weight of the confession.

"Just be there," Bec says simply. Her words are like a balm, soothing and straightforward in their simplicity.

"Bec you don't understand, I'm afraid of dead bodies."

"This is going to make you stronger, Jess, just like every other tough situation you've faced in your life."

I repeat Bec's words to myself, letting them settle into my heart. Maybe that's all I can do. Be there for Martin as he faces the unimaginable. Be there for myself, as I navigate this new and terrifying terrain of grief. There's no guidebook for this, no manual to tell me how to act or what to say. All I can do is be present, hold space for the pain, and to hope that somehow, we can both make it through to the other side.

The decision to confront this fear—the one that has suffocated me for so long—brings a desperate need to face it once and for all.

∗

I PACE THE house, unable to sit still. My phone is glued to my hand, and I keep checking it, waiting for a text that will tell me it's time to go. I feel like a man whose wife is in labour, anxious and impatient, counting down the minutes until I have to confront my trauma.

The phone buzzes, and my heart skips a beat.

We land in five hours.

The clock is ticking. In the next seven hours, I will see a dead body. I don't know what that is going to bring up. A mix of fear, worry and doubts take over. But Bec's words also echo in my mind. I swallow the lump in my throat, push aside my fear, and head to the kitchen. Martin might be hungry, or maybe not, but I cook anyway. I'm grounding myself in the routine. It's something I can control, something tangible in a sea of uncertainty.

I fasten my seatbelt and put a container of fried rice on the seat next to mine. Anxiety claws at me again. I'm to meet Jim, who is part of Martin's family, then drive his car for the trip. I'll also be meeting Max, their employee who I know very little about. This is a new world—Martin's world—and it's moving too fast. But I'm here now, and I can't stop.

My hands grip the steering wheel in Jim's car, trembling slightly as we merge onto the freeway. I've always avoided this road, choosing longer, winding streets over this fast, direct route. A ten-minute drive often turns into forty-five as I take the safer, slower path, trying to keep the shadows at bay. The faster the road, the more chances of encountering danger.

But today, the fear of the freeway is a mere whisper compared to the roar that has been growing since that fateful phone call, gripping my heart with icy fingers as I think about what awaits at the airport.

Jim sits next to me, silent but steady, his presence a small comfort as I navigate through the lanes. The city blurs past while my mind is elsewhere, caught in the tangled web of emotions that have been unravelling since last night.

Perth Airport looms ahead, a sprawling maze of people and movement. As I step out of the car, the world around me turns into a blur. Faces pass by, hurried and indifferent. My focus narrows, every sound muted, every colour dull, until suddenly, there he is.

*

TIME SLOWS AS our eyes meet. He looks different—broken, yet still undeniably Martin. As he walks toward me, something shifts. The world shrinks down to just the two of us, and in that moment, everything else fades away.

He wraps his strong arms around me, and I realise that I'm here for him and he's here for me, too. This is the beginning of something new, painful, and necessary. Martin isn't just walking through his grief—he's leading me back to my own, to face my long-held fears. And for the first time, I feel ready. There is no better person to do it with than this wonderful man standing before me.

He is my hero, and I am his queen. Together, we are about to confront our worst fears, so that we can come out the other side stronger. For a moment, it feels like we're characters in a movie, and the whole world is watching this journey that is about to unfold. The thought of it sends a shiver of anticipation down my spine. Because whatever happens next, we'll face it together. And that, more than anything, gives me the strength to keep going.

Martin raises his head, his eyes scanning the hospital car park as we wait for the others to join us. A woman arrives. The moment Martin sees her, his composure shatters. Before I can even process it, he's moving toward her, their embrace igniting a river of tears between them. It's raw, unfiltered grief. As the rest of the family converges, the emotional dam breaks. This hurts more than I ever imagined.

My feet feel like they're moving on their own, guided by some unseen force, while Martin's strong, masculine hand grips mine, offering a sense of safety in this storm of emotions. I try to ground myself, but the reality of the situation keeps slipping through my fingers. The more we walk, the longer the journey feels, as if the road is doubling in length with each step.

We move from one entry door to another, our voices hushed as we ask for directions, each guide pointing us down a different corridor. It's disorienting, like being trapped in a labyrinth where every turn leads us back to where we started. My thoughts spiral—what if this is a sign for me to turn back? My heart beats faster, the grip on Martin's hand my only anchor. I keep telling myself that he's here, so I'm safe, trying to push through the fear. Martin is here, and he'll protect me. I have to keep moving.

FINALLY, WE ENTER the building that houses the morgue. The air inside is cold and sterile. My mind races as we approach the reception desk, where Martin and the family exchange words with the staff. I stand back, trying to catch my breath as the receptionist gives us directions. "Down the hallway, the third room on your right," she says, her voice calm. My heart flips. A few more steps, and I'll be face-to-face with my deepest fear.

The ground feels like it might give way beneath me. Martin's family continues to speak with the receptionist, but their voices fade into the background as my mind plays out all the possible scenarios. What will Dylan look like? It was a car crash; what if his body is mangled, unrecognisable? What if he's covered in bruises, his skin turning black? Will he be standing, lying down, covered by a sheet? Will we even recognise him? My thoughts spiral out of control, each one darker than the last. Why am I here? This is for adults, not for someone like me. But then again,

I am an adult—a mother of two, for crying out loud. Yet, in this moment, I feel like a frightened child.

"Jess?" Martin's voice pulls me back to reality. I snap out of my trance. For a long moment, we just stare at each other. Martin takes the first step, leading the way, his hand still holding mine. I follow, my feet moving on their own as if they no longer belong to me.

We reach the final barrier between us and Dylan. I pull back, panic rising in my chest. "I can't do this," I whisper, tears spilling over.

Martin turns to me, his eyes softening as he realises the gravity of this moment for me. "Jess, you're with me," he says gently. But the fear is overwhelming, and I shake my head, my body trembling.

"You don't understand, I can't—"

The door creaks open before I can finish, and my eyes shut tight, bracing for what's on the other side. Martin squeezes my hand, his own breath hitching as he steps into the room. I hear him break down, his sobs cutting through the silence. I force myself to open my eyes, and there he is. Dylan. The boy I had pizza with just weeks ago. The boy with the infectious laugh and the bright, curious eyes. Now, he lies motionless, forever frozen in time.

"He's not here," says a family member, his voice heavy, as he takes in the sight of Dylan one last time. "He's gone."

He looks peaceful, like he's just sleeping. His face is calm, undisturbed by the horrors that took him from us. The fear that had been clawing at me vanishes in an instant. I stare at him through the glass, watching as Martin collapses against the barrier, his hands pressed to the surface as if trying to reach his son. My mind races, grappling with the reality of how short the distance between life and death truly is. It's just a breath, a heartbeat, a single moment, and everything changes. We live our lives as if we have all the time in the world, but it's an illusion. In truth, we're all just visitors here, passing through on borrowed time.

Dylan is done with this world. His struggles are over, and he's found peace.

ON THE DRIVE home, the traffic is relentless. Cars rush by as people honk their horns. The world is always in a hurry, always fighting, always chasing something. But for what? What are we really fighting for? Why do we get so comfortable in a place that isn't ours to keep? We're all just passing through, yet we act as if we own the place, building our lives around illusions of permanence.

How foolish we are. How blind. I can't help but feel a deep, aching sadness for all the time we waste, for the battles we fight that mean nothing in the end. We are racing against a clock that doesn't belong to us, and yet, we think we have all the time in the world. We are fools.

CHAPTER 12:
ALONE

DARKNESS BEGINS TO drape over the world, and with it, my fear stirs, rising like an unstoppable tide as we pull into the driveway. Familiar surroundings morph into shadows. As we step out of the car, the slam of doors echo in the stillness. My eyes dart around, scanning every corner. I turn back, once, twice, my gaze sweeping left and right, watching over my shoulders as if the shadows I've imagined for so long are finally closing in, just out of sight and ready to strike at any moment.

The house looms before us, an imposing silhouette against the night sky. We step inside, and the silence is even more deafening here. Every creak of the floorboards, every rustle of fabric seems amplified, as if the house itself is holding its breath. I can feel the weight of the darkness pressing in on me, an unseen force that makes my skin prickle with unease.

✱

LATER, I LIE flat in the bed, the sheets cool against my skin, but there's no comfort in their touch. The room is too quiet. The darkness here is heavy, oppressive stillness. My eyes are wide open, staring into the void above me, searching for something, anything to focus on, but there's only the empty space that seems to stretch on forever.

Beside me, Martin has finally succumbed to exhaustion. His cries have long since quieted, leaving behind only the faint sound of his breath, steady and deep. His arms are wrapped around me, his grip tight, as if I'm his anchor in this sea of grief. Yet, despite his closeness, I feel utterly alone. His warmth should be a comfort, but instead, it only highlights the coldness within me.

I can feel the shadows lurking just beyond the edges of my vision, their presence palpable, ready to pounce the moment I close my eyes. They're not just in my mind anymore—they're here, in this room, in this moment. I've ventured too far, crossed into their territory, and now they're coming for me.

I squeeze my eyes shut, trying to block out the fear, but it only grows stronger, feeding off the silence and the dark. I'm trapped in this room, in this bed, with nothing but my own racing thoughts and the ghosts that haunt them.

"I can't sleep," I whisper, my voice shaky as I turn to look at Martin. His eyes blink open slowly. The clock reads 2:00am in the darkness.

"What can I do to help you sleep?" Martin asks, his voice thick with concern. He reaches out, his hand warm against my cold skin.

"I don't know," I reply, my voice barely above a whisper. The fear has taken root deep inside me, and I feel it spreading, crawling up the walls and pooling in the corners of the room. The shadows seem to move, taking on sinister shapes, and even the large wardrobe mirror across from the bed reflects something I can't quite see but can feel lurking just beyond the glass.

Martin sits up, his brows furrowed in thought. Suddenly, he reaches for something on his nightstand. "Here," he says as he hands me a necklace. The pendant is a small, smooth stone, cool to the touch, strung on a simple black cord.

"A friend gave this to me," he explains as he gently places it around my neck. "They said it's spiritual, that it chases fears away."

I hold the necklace in my hand, its weight comforting against my chest. It reminds me of the good luck charms back home, the ones my grandmother used to make us wear to ward off evil spirits. I thought I had left those superstitions behind, buried with my childhood, but here I am, clinging to this stone as if it's my last hope.

I don't sleep. When sunlight eventually streams through the windows, it does nothing to chase away the lingering fear that's settled in my bones. Martin is gone, back to his routine, and I'm left to face the day alone with just the kids.

By the afternoon, my fear has grown, feeding on the quiet of the house. The walls seem too large and empty. I can't shake the feeling that something is watching, waiting for me to falter. My hands tremble as I try to distract myself with chores, but nothing works.

"M, can you please sleep in my room tonight?" I ask, my voice trembling as I stand in the doorway of my eight-year-old son's room. He looks up from his toys, his innocent eyes filled with confusion.

"Why? Are you scared?" he asks, tilting his head as he studies my face.

"No, not really . . . " I lie, forcing a smile. But he can see through it, and I can see the worry starting to form in his young mind. I hate that I'm doing this to him, dragging him into my fear, but I don't know how to face it alone.

*

The next day, we sit in a small, dimly lit room, the air thick with the smell of incense and something else I can't quite place.

I sit there, numb, as the conversation swirls around me, the words like sharp knives cutting into my consciousness—cremation, ashes, urns, scattering remains. These aren't words meant for my small, fragile mind. They're too big, too final. I feel like a child sitting at a table meant for adults, trying to make sense of a world that's suddenly become too vast, too dark.

I clutch the necklace around my neck, the stone warming from my touch, but it offers no comfort. The fear is still there, a cold presence that refuses to be banished. As the others continue to talk, I stare at the floor, the words sinking deeper into my mind, taking root in the cracks that have started to form.

"These responsibilities are too heavy for me," I say to Martin as we both fasten our seatbelts in the front seats.

"I'm sorry Jess", Martin empathises. "You know, you can take a break."

*

I HAVEN'T SEEN Martin in two days, which seems like two years in our current situation. He's decided to give me space, and as much as I needed that and appreciate him for being thoughtful, a part of me feel very uncomfortable without him. I'm hurting as well, and I feel like it's easier on us with us together. I send him a message, and when he finally shows up at my door, looking like a dead man himself, I realise that life has revealed its beauty and its ugliness, and this is where love is both built and tested.

I never expected that the love which walked into my life less than a year ago would arrive intertwined with loss, grief, and sorrow. And yet, in the midst of it all, I understand something I hadn't before: love is the willingness to stand with beauty and through pain, to witness and hold on, even when the world feels unbearable.

Still, I choose love.

CHAPTER 13:
MISSION ACCOMPLISHED

OUR BLACK LIMOUSINE glides slowly, almost reverently, through the quiet streets. Ahead of us is a white coffin with a bunch of fresh sunflowers resting on top in bright yellow defiance against the sombre world. Inside the limo, Martin and I sit in silence, our hands locked together, sharing strength. My mind is swirling, vivid images and half-formed thoughts crashing together, as if life itself is trying to unfold its mysteries before me.

I don't cry. Somehow, what lies ahead doesn't feel like loss. "It feels like we're seeing Dylan off to the airport," I murmur to Martin, "like he's just completed his mission here. He's gifted us so much, and we're simply watching him board his flight to the other side."

Martin squeezes my hand, his gaze distant and contemplative. "You're right. It does feel like that," he says softly.

A memory of Mummy, inconsolable at Father's death, comes flooding back. She was wailing like her heart was splitting open, telling us that she saw him boarding a plane in a dream the night before he died.

In this moment, something deeper stirs. It's a powerful force, unseen but undeniable, wrapping itself around us all. The one thing I've feared all my life—death—is now here, and yet, I feel an unexpected peace, calm like I've never known. I think back to Dylan's family at the mortuary, saying, "He's not here. He's gone." The soul has left the body. This form we mourn over was just a vessel, a beautiful shell, housing something far greater. The body was never more than a temporary home.

As we make our way through the cemetery, surrounded by thousands of silent graves, a realisation takes hold of me. Each life, no matter how brief or grand, had its purpose. Each one completed a mission, leaving behind traces of love, pain, laughter—pieces of a life fully lived. The fear I once carried melts away.

The limo stops, and we step out, the air thick with the scent of flowers and freshly turned soil. Martin and the other men lift the coffin, carrying it gently to where the ceremony will begin. I walk behind, determined to capture every moment. This is a memory I want to hold on to.

The ceremony is simple but overflowing with friends, family, teachers and neighbours. They gather tightly, shoulder to shoulder, filling every inch of space. There's a quiet reverence as we stand together, bound by the loss of Dylan. I look around, taking in the faces of those he touched. In their eyes, I see reflections of him—a life lived fully, though far too briefly.

* MISSION ACCOMPLISHED

One by one, people step forward to share stories, their words drifting through the cool evening air. A friend speaks of his kindness and his parents share his dreams with the rest of us. Dylan may have only been sixteen, but he left behind something more meaningful than many do in a lifetime. He lived a full, rich life with purpose, and a depth of love that many never reach. I realise that the way Dylan lived is the whole point of having a life.

Candles surround his white coffin as we step forward to say our final goodbyes. Flames soften the stillness, their light catching on bouquets of wildflowers which rest around him, as vibrant and delicate as the life they honour. They will wither over time, leaving only seeds behind.

As the ceremony nears its end, Dylan's coffin begins its slow descent. The candles shimmer, and in that moment, an unexpected calm washes over me, a sudden understanding that feels both surreal and deeply comforting. Death, I realise, is not an ending but a transition, a journey that carries us across worlds. Just as cars and planes take us from place to place, death transports us to somewhere beyond.

Everything around us—the ticking wall clocks, the birds soaring above, the people gathered here—they're all vessels of meaning. Life, I realise, is a journey of interpreting these meanings, of finding the hidden messages in the ordinary, in the connections we make and the love we share.

CHAPTER 14:
CALLING

WEEKS HAVE SLIPPED by since Dylan's burial, yet the empty space he has left remains as tangible as my own skin. Grief has settled into me like a second heartbeat. It feels like I'm living beneath a heavy cloud, tethered to the sorrow by an invisible string I cannot cut. I find myself lingering at the edge of this space, suspended between life and loss, waiting for something that will allow me to move forward.

It never comes. Instead, I am forced to confront the vastness of this ache, and it isn't only Dylan's passing I feel. It is the ungrieved losses I have been carrying with me: my godmother, Uncle Ifeanyi, Uncle Patrick, my brother, my father. I don't know if this is ever going to end.

Running helps sometimes. There's a narrow trail that winds through a nearby park, where trees bow overhead like silent witnesses to my struggle and the cool air bites at my skin, waking me up. On a morning like any other, I am running as Dylan's face flashes before me; his bright eyes, his unruly blonde curls, his smile—a fragment of pure sunlight breaking through the gloom.

The sight staggers me, my legs nearly giving way as tears blur my vision. His memory crashes into me with such force that I find myself calling friends—Kerryn, Preetie, Bec—trying to untangle this strange grief that grips me, trying to understand why his passing has hollowed me out like this.

"Why him? Why am I suffering so much?" The questions spill out over the phone, hanging there, raw and unanswered. I barely knew Dylan; he was just a boy I met through his father. Yet his loss has carved something out of me, leaving an ache that feels ancient, as if it's rooted deep within my soul. Every attempt at release brings his memory rushing back, as though he's etched into me, a part of my very being.

Responsibilities pile up, tasks that once felt urgent but now seem pointless in the face of this new understanding. I was supposed to start university again; just months ago, the idea thrilled me. Now, it feels like an insurmountable weight. "I'm not sure I can take on any units this semester," I tell my supervisor. They offer understanding, though I see the quiet confusion in their eyes.

Martin senses the shift in me. One evening, sitting across from him, I find myself saying, "I need help." He reaches for my hand. "I'm sorry for pulling you into all of this," he says softly. "But I'm also grateful, because even in his short time, I can see that Dylan left an impression on you, like he did with so many other people."

I nod. Life has shifted irrevocably, and no words seem enough to mend the gap. I drift through my days, watching others rush through life, always busy, always striving. But from where I stand now, it all seems empty. What are we all chasing? What are we rushing toward?

In the stillness of my room, a thought stirs. It's faint at first, then louder, insistent; a call that won't be silenced.

Words are coming at me from every corner, too many to process, each one demanding attention. I don't have time for this, I think, brushing it off, pushing it aside. But then one voice comes, clear and persistent. It says, "*You are called.*"

There's no escaping it, no outrunning what's been chasing me all this time. The pieces click into place, finally. All the things that have haunted me—the fear of death, the move to Australia, my passion for filmmaking, my drive to understand the importance of our gifts—they're all connected. I've been circling around this truth, unknowingly, for years. And now, it's here, staring me down, refusing to let me go. The voice in my heart grows louder. I stop resisting.

And then, I begin to listen. Really listen. The words flow through me, each one feeling like a revelation. When I share these things with others, they get goosebumps. I get goosebumps. Part of me wants to stop. It feels too big, too much. But it won't let me. I can't move on until I share what I've learned.

I write, letting the words spill onto the page. I'm no longer the one holding the pen; something else guides me. I can feel it.

*

I HAD A vision. I saw God, vast as the sky, as a white lion, his presence filling the clouds. But he was sad, disappointed that we're missing the point, lost in the rush of trivial things. I woke up stunned, unable to make sense of it. But two days later, at a theatre performance, I watched my vision play out on stage, almost frame by frame. I was shaken, ran home, and told my kids, "We're going to Church." And they looked at me, confused. "What's Church?"

That day, in Church, I heard the story of the Samaritan woman, which teaches that God tries to reach the world through people's gifts. It hit me: I'm a speaker, I stand on stage and connect with hundreds of people. I realised that my voice was given to me for a reason. God is trying to pass his messages through me. All of my challenges, all of my struggles are part of my purpose. Deep down, I had always known what it was: to remind people that they, too, carry their own purpose, and like mine, it is far greater than they can imagine in the beginning of their lives. But after witnessing death and loss up close, the urgency of that calling has sharpened for me. Time is short. None of us know how much we have left.

All of this revelation made me realised that somebody has been watching me all along, and that none of all of the things that I have faced were a coincidence. "I think this was why we met," I say to Martin.

"I hope there are other reasons," he replies.

CHAPTER 15:
LIFE & MEANING

BIRTH BRINGS US into this world, life is the journey where we deliver our message, and death is the way we return to where we came from. In this light, death is not a loss, but the fulfillment of our task. It is a homecoming after a long, purposeful journey. And that journey, with all its twists and turns, its pain and joy, was always leading us to delivery, and then to rest.

This understanding doesn't erase the sorrow of loss or the fear of the unknown, but it reframes it in a way that gives meaning to the inevitable. It's the natural order of things, a cycle as old as time. And in that, there is beauty, grace and peace.

There's a quiet sense of completion that has settled into my bones, as if a puzzle that had always been missing pieces has finally come together. This knowledge has grounded and tethered me to something so vast and unshakeable that the rush and scramble of the world feels small by comparison.

For the first time, I feel a release from the endless chase. I am here, exactly where I need to be. The pressure to become something or someone other than who I already am has lifted. I am free, and in this freedom, there is a sense of fulfilment so complete that I no longer feel the need to fear death. Once an ominous shadow, death now feels like an inevitable reunion, a gentle return to the force that placed me here. My attention is on the life I've been given and on what I've come here to do. My task is simply to live it with open hands and an open heart.

I feel abundance flow through me like a steady river, clear and sure. My steps are lighter, my voice carries differently. Everything reflects this inner wholeness. I am no longer in competition with anyone, not even with myself. There's nothing to prove, nothing to grasp at.

Life feels richer, yet simpler. I find myself working less, no longer driven by the need to accomplish or accumulate. Instead, I am drawn to what truly matters: moments with family, laughter with friends, the quiet joy of being fully present. These are the things that make each day feel like a gift. I am more loving, more open, letting my time and energy flow only into what resonates with this purpose that guides me.

Even my work has transformed. It's no longer just business; it's become a way of pouring myself into the world from a deep place of truth. My work has become the sheer joy of giving wholeheartedly, without reservation.

When I penned my first book, *I'm Not a Nurse,* I believed that the story had reached its natural conclusion, just as a hero's journey ends with resolution. I thought my journey was complete. I didn't realise that the end of one story often marks the beginning of another. For a storyteller like me, the narrative must continue to unfold.

For the last ten years, my mentor would ask me, "How's your world?" Each time, I would spend the next hour pouring out the details of my life. When I finally noticed the time and apologised for going on too long, he'd simply say, "My life is boring; I live vicariously through yours." Only now do I fully grasp what he meant. I've been blessed with an abundance of stories because I am, at my core, a storyteller. And a storyteller always needs a story to tell.

AFTERWORD

THE SOUL IS a traveller; ancient, knowing, and purposeful. The body, for all its marvels, is not the pilot. Once vibrant with motion and laughter, the body in death reveals its truth: it was never more than the temporary home where a soul resided.

It's unsettling to realise how easily we forget that we are souls animating flesh. A vehicle can't steer itself. Aliveness, personality and radiance are all owed to the soul. Without it, the body is no more than a well-woven garment, hung up after navigating this physical plane for a brief, divine mission.

When I first began writing this chapter, my ex-father-in-law, Gordon, was still alive. As I write these words now, he has crossed over. I witnessed his final days, beside his bed with my ex-mother-in-law, who had been his partner in love and life for over sixty years. She held his hand gently as she reminded him of all their moments: holidays, laughs, children, storms weathered. At that point, all he could do was nod. I gave them their space and quietly left. Not even an hour later, I got the call. He was gone.

"He just went peacefully," my mother-in-law said, her voice cracking. "He didn't make a sound. I was talking to him, and when I looked up, he had gone." It startled her, how suddenly life slipped into silence. That thin veil between life and death is more transparent than we think.

We are not meant to cling to those who must leave. The children and I sat in the room with Gordon's body, but this time, I felt no fear. My ex-father-in-law simply looked like he was sleeping.

As a child, I couldn't even say the word "dead". It felt like an invitation; like if I uttered it, Death would come. The mystery around it made it darker. It wasn't just unknown, it was taboo. No one around me had answers. Not the adults. Not the elders. No one could explain where people went when they died, even though every single one of us would eventually go there. I longed for just a hint, something to ease the fear. If a nurse gives you an injection, they warn you, "It'll sting a little." That warning makes all the difference. But death? No warnings. No map. No reassurance. Just silence.

I won't pretend I know exactly where the dead go. I don't. But I do know that birth and death are part of the same thread. We arrive one way and depart the other. The real question isn't "What happens after we die?" but rather, "Why are we here?"

Think of it like this: if you booked a flight to Mexico, you'd be going for a reason. Maybe work, maybe a holiday, maybe healing. You also wouldn't plan to stay forever. You'd book a return ticket. Just like that, your soul chose to enter a body with an intention and a time to return in mind. Earth is not your permanent home. It's your Mexico. A place of growth during your temporary residence. And just as you'd book an AirBnB or hotel to stay in while you're in Mexico, your soul has rented your body for the duration of its mission.

* AFTERWORD

This is the Soul's Circle: arrival, mission, departure. And while the body ages, decays, and returns to the dust, the soul continues its journey. Always.

We often ask, "Why did someone so young have to go?" But that question assumes that life is about how long each of us stays, rather than what each of us do while we're here.

Some souls only need to enter briefly. Impact doesn't always require longevity.

So, forget the distractions. Forget the comparisons. Focus on what brought you here. You've already been born. You've already picked a body to move around in. Now ask: why this body? Why this life?

If your soul came wearing a police uniform, it's probably here to bring justice, protect, and uphold truth. If your suit looks like a nurse's scrub, maybe you're here to heal, comfort, or hold space for the sick. Don't try to be a singer if your soul signed up to be a surgeon. Don't take the fish out of the water.

Our time here is short. Our return flight is already booked. Let's make it count.

PIECES
OF ME

BY MARTIN SOKLICH
MY PIECE OF HIM—A FATHER'S REFLECTION

MY NAME'S MARTIN, and I'm Dylan's dad. Even now, those words sit heavy in my heart. Never in my wildest dreams did I imagine I'd be the one telling his story like this. I always thought I'd be the one to go first. I pictured being here to watch him find his place in the world, growing into a man of strength, heart and character on his way to make his mark. I imagined seeing how he'd shape the world that was laid out before him.

I never once imagined a life without Dylan. Not for a single second.

Dylan was the kind of kid who made people feel something just by being near him. As a little boy, he was the sweetest thing you could ever meet; quiet at first, but once he opened up, his joy was infectious. When Dylan laughed, he had this energy that would burst through. He'd chuckle, he'd giggle, he'd totally lose control and you couldn't help but laugh with him. He was just something else.

He was such a happy, energetic little boy. The fun and energy he had as a toddler carried right through to his early school years. A sweet-faced and beautiful boy, with a gorgeous lock of hair that became such a part of who he was. Dylan was never any trouble; just a cool little kid with a big heart, and a way of leaving people better than he found them.

There was a gentleness about him, a way of watching people and feeling what they felt. Even as a little boy, he could walk into a room and somehow know who needed a hug. His emotional intelligence was far beyond his years. While most of us were still trying to figure out how to handle our own storms, Dylan had already found his centre.

That sensitivity showed itself early. If you told him off, or spoke with just a touch more sternness than usual, his eyes would well up. It wasn't because he was weak, it was because he felt things so deeply and instantly. He was in tune with the people around him in a way you rarely see, especially in a child.

Wherever we went, he'd hang off my side. He wanted to be close, and I loved that. When Dylan held onto me, I could feel the love pouring out of him. It was intense, but in the most beautiful way. Some people might have said he was a bit clingy, but that was just Dylan showing love. And it made me feel so good inside, like I was the safest, most loved person on Earth.

Dylan had a way of losing himself in his own world. He was never short of ways to keep busy. He loved playing outside, and gymnastics quickly became a defining passion. He pushed himself to try new things, whether it was swinging on the bars, doing splits, handstands, or running through his routines. He'd go at it all day. It was his way of throwing himself into something and completely losing himself in the moment. He loved it.

✱ MY PIECE OF HIM—A FATHER'S REFLECTION

As he moved into his teens, his sensitivity became his greatest power. It was a strength most people will never truly understand, let alone possess. It wasn't fragile, it was fierce. If kids teased him, or if life threw something at him that didn't go his way, Dylan didn't just stand his ground; he owned it. He carried himself with a calm authority that made others stop and take notice. What had once been his tender spot became this unshakable core, a strength so natural and so rare that it left a lasting impression on everyone who crossed his path.

People often thought he was shy at first, but really, he was just reading them, assessing who they were and what they were bringing. It's part of the gift he gave to those around him, and why he left such a mark on people's hearts.

Dylan was different: he was sensitive, alternative, and unafraid to see the world in his own way. He thought differently, looked differently, acted differently. He navigated his challenges with a quiet determination that made me the proudest dad. He had this fantastic light inside him, guiding him forward, and even in difficult times, his dreams were never far from his mind.

He found a fantastic group of friends who accepted him for exactly who he was. He realised that it didn't matter what anyone else thought, as long as he was himself. Once he embraced that freedom, he really shone. He was warm, approachable, and had a knack for making people feel comfortable straight away. His friendliness and quiet confidence made him easy to be around, and it wasn't long before he became known as the friend everyone liked having close by.

When I got the call that Dylan had passed, I was overseas. I'd been out picking up a few gifts and treats for my boys and Jessica. I always picked up Sour Patch lollies for Dylan when I went to the United States, but this time when I reached for them on the shelf, something startled me. Clear as day, I heard his voice say, "Don't worry about me, Dad. I'm okay." I can't explain it, but there was a strong, certain feeling that I should put them back.

In my mind, I thought about the health kick Dylan had been on recently. In my heart, I know it was simply him speaking to me.

Barely an hour after that moment with the Sour Patch lollies, my phone rang. It was the call that changed everything.

By the time I made it back to Perth, the truth had already settled deep inside me. When I finally saw his body, still and lifeless, it was confirmed. His soul was no longer there. His body was just a vessel. He was free.

I had been distraught; broken in a way I'd never known before, but as I sat down beside him, there was a strange sense of calm and comfort that I couldn't explain. I just knew he'd moved on peacefully. I could feel him. His presence filled the room, and his hand rested on my shoulder. I've felt that same touch many times since.

Grief does strange things to you. It shatters you, but in the middle of that wreckage, something else can grow; a new awareness, a deeper love. Dylan left a hole in my life so big it can never be filled, but he also left pieces of himself behind. Dylan lived with heart, and now I want to do the same, by creating something meaningful and helping other young people find what Dylan had: that deep knowing of who they are, even when the world doesn't always understand. I'm no longer focused on chasing money or status the way I once did.

Jessica and I have been walking this journey together. Her grief, her wisdom, and her belief in the soul's journey have helped carry me through. She was there by my side, and Dylan's passing affected her deeply too. Jessica believes Dylan is still here, just in a different form, and honestly, so do I.

There's no other way to explain how often he shows up. In the quiet moments, if I start questioning myself or wondering if I'm imagining it, another sign appears, clear as day. It's like being tapped on the shoulder or slapped in the face.

We're not out to save the world, but we are out to love it better, to create something that lasts, and to offer a piece of Dylan to others through genuine connection. Dylan has sparked a new fire in me. I know this part of me is his gift. In just sixteen years, he gave more to the world than many manage in a much longer life. His legacy lives in every person he touched and in every choice I now make.

Dylan was inspired by his own discovery of who he was. Out of these struggles, he established a business called *Just You Cosmetics*. It wasn't just a brand name for him, it was about embodying his beliefs. If there's one thing I can pass on from him, it's this; you—*Just You*—are enough. That's what he knew, and that's how he lived.

To have known him will forever be one of my greatest memories.

I love you, Boy.

(In their eyes, I live)

Dylan Soklich

Our beloved boy Dylan
We will miss you mate
Gone, But Not Forgotten
Sending all my love
Miss you gorgeous
You put a smile on every ones face
Best Dancer OUT!!
We all love & support you
Amelia I love you forever
We are always here for you if you need - Justin Harrap
we will miss you
SLAY Dyldog I miss you
Social Butterfly Miss you Lots
Light in the dark, Bright little spark
Will forever miss his beautiful smile, And his amazing & funny soul & personality
I love you so much dylan and I will forever miss you x

www.ingramcontent.com/pod-product-compliance
Lightning Source LLC
Chambersburg PA
CBHW031254290426
44109CB00012B/572